The 'Plan For America'

How to Place the American Dream on a Sure
Foundation Forever

Terry Nager, CFP®, ChFC®, CLU®

Eric Nager, CRPS®

Kyre Lahtinen, PhD

Plan For America®

V-9

ISBN: 978-1-945190-89-6

Cover artwork by Andrea Hunt.

Published by: Intellect Publishing, LLC

www.IntellectPublishing.com

Dedication

To every U.S. Citizen, present and future:
you are the heroes of this story.

Acknowledgments

In working on this plan over many years, quite a few people
helped us along the way. We want to gratefully acknowledge
them here: David Holmes, Ernie Berger, Bob Callahan, Sr.,
Ted Greenspan, Tim Swanson,
Dr. Ross Dickens, Nancy Busey, Rocky Wells Mark Nager,
Kristi Hunt, Breana Gaines, Joshua Hunt, Andrea Hunt,
Michelle Hunt, Chris Nager, Charlotte Straight, Ashleigh
Donnelly, Wendy Nelson Bailey, David Lindsey, Paul Nager,
Ted Burnett, C.J. Ezell, Sandy Nager and
John O'Melveny Woods.

TEN EMN

I wish to thank my family for their never-ending support.

KDL

Table of Contents

Introduction

The American Dream is still alive.

At one time that meant a married couple with good jobs, two children, a house in the suburbs with a picket fence, and two cars in the garage. Over time that definition has broadened, but the American Dream has basically always meant that every citizen in the United States has an opportunity for a good quality of life.

Unspoken in that promise is a comfortable retirement with adequate income and quality healthcare. Historically, a pension funded that retirement and the employer provided healthcare. The typical American worker spent his whole career in one job and retired with the proverbial gold watch and a pension, or monthly payment based on his salary and years of service, for life.

That is no longer the case. Most Americans change jobs multiple times in their careers and most employers no longer offer pensions. But the Dream is still underpinned by Social Security and Medicare, right? Unfortunately, no.

We will get into the financial problems facing our nation in the first chapter. Many Americans have a retirement plan through work, like a 401(k), that can help support them in retirement. In fact, hard work has been the key to securing the American Dream for generations.

After the Greatest Generation returned from winning World War II, they went back to school and work and helped usher in the greatest sustained economic boom the world has ever seen. Since then, innovative advances in technology and productivity have continued to increase our national standard of living. Look no further than the recent example of hydraulic fracking that made the U.S. go from a net importer to exporter of energy and helped us dig out of the Great Recession of 2008-2009.

Behind all of this success, prosperity, and progress stands the American worker. In exchange for a lifetime of sacrifice, sweat, and success, he and she deserve the opportunity for a worry-free retirement where there is no threat of the retirement system running out of money and there is freedom to pursue happy activities such as spending time with grandchildren to traveling or volunteering.

Throughout Part I of this book, we will be looking at Plan For America through the eyes of a hero: a single mother who lives in an inner city. She works hard her whole career and will only have Social Security and Medicare in retirement. What legacy will she be able to leave her heirs?

The American worker is a hero who has earned the right to carefree golden years. The aim of this book is to restore that vision and to place the American Dream on a sure foundation forever. There is still time, but we must act quickly.

Will you join us on this important journey?

The 'Plan For America'

How to Place the American Dream on a Sure Foundation Forever

Part I

What Plan For America Does

www.PlanForAmerica.us

Chapter 1

Debts and Deficits

Alas, all is not well in the Land of Plenty. For years the U.S. Government has spent more than it has taken in, resulting in annual deficits. For the fiscal year ending in September of 2020, that deficit was projected to be about $1 trillion *before* the SARS-CoV-2 crisis. After the crisis, that deficit is estimated to be close to $4 trillion and counting.

On top of annual deficits, that now cumulatively total about $23.3 trillion, there is something called unfunded liabilities. These are obligations the U.S. Government has to recipients of Social Security and Medicare beyond the government's expected revenues. These liabilities are estimated to be about $120 trillion.

Before we continue, let's quantify how much a trillion is because most of us do not deal with numbers this large in daily life so it can be hard to imagine how much we are really talking about here. Most of us are familiar with a $100 bill. If you had a packet of 100 of these bills, you would have $10,000, which would fit into your pocket. If you had 100 such packets, you would have $1 million, which would still fit easily into a shopping bag. If you had 100 of these bags, you would have $100 million, or about the size of a regular pallet. Ten of those pallets would give you $1 billion. But to get to one trillion, you would need a football field filled with *double stacked* pallets. One hundred trillion would fill 100 football fields.

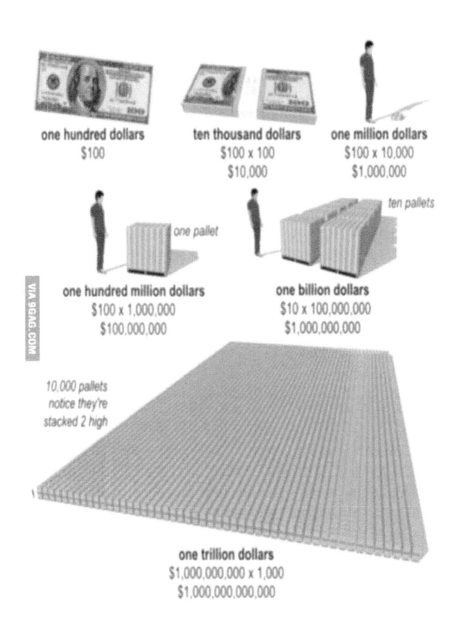

one hundred dollars
$100

ten thousand dollars
$100 x 100
$10,000

one million dollars
$100 x 10,000
$1,000,000

one pallet

ten pallets

one hundred million dollars
$100 x 1,000,000
$100,000,000

one billion dollars
$10 x 100,000,000
$1,000,000,000

10,000 pallets
notice they're
stacked 2 high

one trillion dollars
$1,000,000,000 x 1,000
$1,000,000,000,000

Now that you have an idea of the magnitude of the problem the natural question is, how did we get into this mess? The answer is that a villain has been on the loose. That villain is the U.S. politician of both parties, who has failed spectacularly to serve

While most politicians enter politics with noble motives, there is an old saying that "power corrupts, but absolute power corrupts absolutely."

his customer, the U.S. Citizen. While most politicians enter politics with noble motives to help others, there is an old saying that "power corrupts, and absolute power corrupts absolutely."

In order to get re-elected, the politician's ultimate goal, he or she will make promises that cannot be kept. The consequences of not keeping the promise do not fall onto the politician because the promise is made to land on future generations, long after the politician is out of office. The term that comes to mind for this is "Ponzi scheme." A Ponzi scheme is defined as "a form of fraud in which belief in the success of a nonexistent enterprise is fostered by payment of quick returns to the first investors from money invested by later investors." Let's look at some of those broken promises through the lens of our entitlement programs.

Social Security

Social Security was enacted in the 1930s as a social safety net during a time of economic depression. At that time, the typical American life expectancy was about 67 years and there were 30-40 workers contributing per retiree who was drawing benefits. The politicians promised that benefits would not be taxable. The Payroll tax rate for individuals was 1% of their pay, matched by employers, and full retirement age was 65.

Today, all those rules have been changed and the demographics of our society have shifted. Life expectancy is now about a decade longer and there are only 2-3 workers supporting each retiree. Instead of adjusting benefits to take this into account, the politicians promised more. Today Social Security benefits are potentially taxable, and the Social Security payroll tax rate has grown to 6.2% of earnings, matched by the employer. The full retirement age has been raised to 67 for those born after 1960.

All of these changes have put pressure on the system, making it unsustainable for the long run. According to *The Wall Street Journal,* projected benefits will start to exceed revenues in 2021. The trustees for Social Security estimate that the trust funds will be depleted in 2035 and after that, if no changes are made, they will only be able to pay out 79% of scheduled benefits ("Pandemic Takes Toll on Social Security," Kate Davidson, April 23, 2020).

At least we have a long time to make changes to the system since there is still plenty of money in the trust fund, right? Wrong. The Social Security trust fund is depleted NOW. The villainous politicians raided it long ago and spent it on other things. So instead of your payroll taxes being earmarked just for you sometime in the future, the government spent that money and replaced it with a non-negotiable IOU. Non-negotiable means it cannot be traded or converted to cash without government borrowing. In other words, the only way for the government to get money to redeem the IOUs is to borrow more money. So, in reality, the Social Security system is broke now, not in 2035.

Medicare and Medicaid

As bad as the Social Security problem is, it is only about 15% of the trillions in unfunded liabilities owed by the government. The lion's share of the debts and deficits come from Medicare and Medicaid. These two programs were part of the Great Society reforms of the 1960s and, like Social Security, the promises have been broken by the politicians.

As a refresher, Medicare is the program that takes care of seniors starting at age 65. It is really a healthcare supplement in the sense it does not pay for everything. For example, it does not cover all prescription drugs or hearing aids and it only covers a very limited amount of nursing home care.

Medicaid is a program for the poor who cannot afford coverage. Once someone has spent her entire means, she can go on Medicaid and have that cover her nursing home care, for example. You are only eligible for this program if you have almost no assets to support you.

Medicare takes 2.9% of your payroll taxes. You pay 1.45% and this is matched by your employer. In other words, this program,

Taken together, Social Security, Medicare, and Medicaid really do fit the definition of a Ponzi scheme.

which is way more expensive than Social Security, takes far less of your payroll taxes to support it. And, with medical costs far outpacing inflation over the past decades, it is no wonder that the debts associated with Medicare have gotten out of hand. Unbelievably, a proposal by some politicians in this election cycle is to expand the program and create "Medicare for all." How responsible is that?

Taken together, Social Security, Medicare, and Medicaid really do fit the definition of a Ponzi scheme in that younger workers (the latest "investors") who are paying into the system are funding today's retirees. When these younger workers reach retirement age themselves, the promised benefits will not be there for them unless there are significant changes. Many politicians have proposed band-aid solutions, but nothing that will permanently solve the problem.

One possible, partial solution is to raise the retirement age. After all, U.S. Citizens are living longer. But merely raising the age by which one becomes eligible to receive benefits will only delay, and not solve the debt crisis.

How just would it be to pay into a system your entire life and get very little or nothing in return?

Likewise, another proposal is to "means test" benefits. In other words, those of means, or financial support, yet to be defined, would be ineligible to receive benefits. Aside from the fact that, in order to be a meaningful reform, only the very poor would stand to get benefits, there is an issue of fairness. How just would it be to pay into a system your entire life and get very little or nothing in return? In either case, neither raising the eligibility age nor means testing will actually pay down the debt. These measures would only allow a broken system to limp along a few extra years.

The States

Unfortunately, the federal entitlement programs are not the only debt problem our nation faces. Many U.S. states are also in dangerous financial situations. This issue is partly masked by the fact that most state constitutions require state budgets to be balanced. Most states cannot run deficits like the federal government, but the problem is there nonetheless. It is also masked by the fact that the federal government provides a significant portion of state budgets through Medicaid payments. Without them, most states would be bleeding red ink.

The other main driver of potential state debts is guaranteed pensions for state employees like teachers and firefighters. While no one would argue these are not noble professions deserving of excellent compensation, unaccountable politicians have gotten in the way again, as usual. Public employees are an important voting block and, in order to win votes, politicians in many states have promised retirement benefits to these workers that their states cannot afford. Those under-funded pensions are yet another unfunded liability that will come home to roost if drastic action is not taken.

In summary, our nation's debt of all types is a crisis that cannot be avoided without change. Currently the entitlement programs take about two-thirds of government spending, and growing. At some point, they will crowd out all discretionary spending, including defense spending for our nation's military, making this issue one of national security. Government debt also crowds out more productive use of

> *Unfunded (state) pensions are yet another unfunded liability that will come home to roost if drastic action is not taken.*

capital in private equity markets. The debt is a giant boulder hanging over our collective heads and threatening to crush us. At some point the government will lose the ability to pay and many Americans will be left without retirement or health benefits. You do not want to be one of those Americans. Something needs to be done now.

Summary of Chapter One:

- Our country is well over $100 trillion in debt and a trillion dollars is a football field full of double stacked pallets of $100 bills.

- Like a Ponzi scheme, the politicians have raided the Social Security and Medicare trust funds so that they are broke NOW.

- States are crushed by Medicaid and unfunded pension liabilities.

Chapter 2

Meet Your Guides

All three authors of this book are parents. The main motivation in writing this and coming up with a solution to our national debt crisis is that we want our children and future grandchildren to have the same opportunities we have enjoyed growing up in this country. We still believe that the United States is the land of opportunity and we do not want to see that vision wiped out in a cloud of debt and uncertainty.

Already there is pessimism. The millennial generation, roughly those aged 20-40, and Generation Z, those 20 and younger, generally do not have confidence that their lives will be better than those of their parents. Count us as optimists that with the right vision and planning, this country can see its way through any crisis to prosper and thrive.

Terry Nager is the principal author of our plan and wrote Part II of this book. He is President of Southern Capital Services, an investment advisory firm, and his main credential is that of a Certified Financial Planner, or CFP®. He has held that designation for 40 years and has been in the financial services industry for 45 years. He also holds the credentials of Chartered Life Underwriter, or CLU®, and Chartered Financial Consultant, or ChFC®.

Once he became an empty nester, Terry started thinking about our national debt crisis. He asked himself, "What would

11

be a reasonably comprehensive financial plan for every American citizen?" A comprehensive financial plan includes the areas of insurance, taxes, investments, estate planning, and retirement and he has drawn upon his years of experience working with his clients to devise that aspect of Plan For America.

Eric Nager wrote Part I of this book. He has been working with Terry at Southern Capital Services for the past 20 years and holds the designation of Chartered Retirement Plans Specialist, or CRPS®. This credential gives him perspective on how individual accounts work within 401k and other types of retirement plans. Eric earned his MBA from the University of South Alabama and a Masters in history from Harvard.He had a brief career in politics as a city councilman and he served our country in uniform for 30 years as a member of the U.S. Army Reserve.

Dr. Kyre Lahtinen is a professor of economics at Wright State University in Ohio and wrote Part III of this book. He earned his doctoral degree from Florida State University and he is the author of the econometric model that was used to vet Plan For America. This model was built in conformity with Congressional Budget Office (CBO) and Social Security Administration (SSA) assumptions, so the plan "speaks the same language" as the politicians, so to speak, despite the limitations that come with that.

Work on this plan started after the election of 2004 when President George W. Bush proposed a partial privatization of Social Security. At the time, we were coming off the recession of 2000-2002 and his plan was denounced because there was no guaranteed return and the market had crashed. Still, it got Terry to thinking in new directions and since then the plan has been revised and improved. Now that we are in the midst of the SARS-CoV-2 financial crisis, we feel that the timing for this plan has never been better. Allow us to be your guides as we now explain what Plan For America does.

Summary of Chapter Two:

- **Plan For America is a financial plan for each citizen.**

- **Terry is a Certified Financial Planner, CFP®, with 45 years of experience in the financial services industry**

- **Eric is a Chartered Retirement Plans Specialist, CRPS®, with 20 years of experience.**

- **Kyre holds a PhD in economics and finance.**

Chapter 3

Plan For America

This chapter will explain what our plan does. In order to understand how the plan works, we have devoted an entire section of this book to questions and answers, and another that explains the numbers. We realize that not everyone wants to know how something works. When I start my car, for example, I am not concerned about how an internal combustion engine works. I just want to get to my destination.

In this case, the hero's destination is a debt-free America. To arrive there, we have devised a plan unlike any other we have seen. What makes our plan unique is a *funding mechanism,* or a way to actually pay off and retire all state and federal debts. In fact, our plan will eventually replace taxation of every type as a way to fund government.

Another aspect of the plan is that the benefits it will give to those who participate in it are *far better* than those that one would receive from Social Security and Medicare. Politicians love to scare voters by claiming that their opponents will "cut" or "take away" their Social Security or healthcare. But if Social Security is replaced by a better, more secure retirement and Medicare is replaced by better, more comprehensive healthcare, that is nothing to be frightened about. Instead, changes should be welcomed because the politicians keep changing the rules about the entitlement programs.

Remember, the current path is NOT sustainable. That is why tweaks to the current system will not work. They only delay the inevitable crash of the system. In the last chapter we referred to President Bush's idea to look at partially privatizing Social Security. He was ripped to pieces because we had just come through a recession and people's retirement accounts had dropped along with the market. To solve that dilemma, our plan offers a *guaranteed rate of return* to participants, regardless of market performance.

> *Our plan offers a guaranteed rate of return to participants, regardless of market performance.*

Yet another feature of our plan is that it offers high quality, affordable healthcare to *every U.S. Citizen.* When the so-called Affordable Care Act went into effect under President Obama, it was touted as covering more Americans than any other plan ever has, but even Obamacare left out somewhere between 20-40 million Americans. Plan For American leaves out no one since it is truly universal.

Establishing our plan has an added measure of security: we propose to enact the plan through *contract law,* not just legislation. Legislation can be changed when congress and the presidency change hands from one party to another. A contract is much more difficult to change and sets Plan For America on firmer footing.

We know what you are thinking: all of this sounds too good to be true. And when something sounds too good to be true, it usually is. In this case, all of the promised goodies are possible because we have one more thing on our side: the power of compounding that Albert Einstein called the "eighth wonder of the world." As a quick aside, let's review how compounding works with small numbers and that will serve to illustrate the larger point.

Establishing our plan has an added measure of security: we propose to enact the plan through contract law, not just legislation.

One of our favorite ways to illustrate compound interest is with an investment example. Let's say a saver invested $200 per month from age 25 to age 65. After 40 years he would have set aside $96,000. Now let's say another saver invested $400 per month from age 45 to 65. After 20 years, he would also have set aside $96,000. If each got an 8-9% average annual rate of return, who would do better and would it really make that much difference?

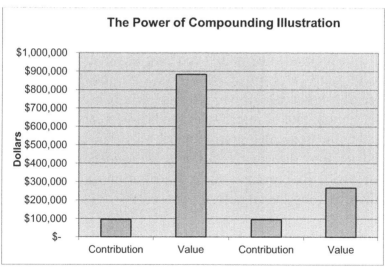

According to the graph, the one who saved earlier would have more than three times the amount as the saver who waited, because he had 20 extra years of compounding working for him. From this illustration you can see what a powerful tool compounding interest is, and it is this tool we are harnessing to work on behalf of Plan For America.

Retirement

Now let's go back to the contract since that has to happen first in order for the plan to go into effect. While the contract would have to be enabled by legislation, the contract itself would be among the federal government, the state governments, and a private trust to be established by the contract. The name of the trust is the **For America Security Trust**, or FAST. Once the trust comes into being, each American Citizen, at your option, could elect to divert the 15.3% payroll tax you are currently paying to Social Security and Medicare into a private account in your name in the FAST, not unlike a 401k plan. After all, this is YOUR money! (Let's call this Goody #1.)

This money would then be invested in an all market index of publicly traded U.S. companies. An index fund is virtually costless because there is no management: it just holds the stocks of companies in the index. This would allow you to get market returns, which would far exceed Social Security (Goody #2). According to Morningstar/Ibbotson, a prestigious statistical source of market data, the market as a whole has averaged about 10.2% annual rate of return over the last 94 years. As part of the contract, the federal government agrees that all contributions would go into the trust tax-deductible and come out tax-free (Goody #3). By contrast, 401k contributions are tax-deductible but distributions are taxable.

Upon retirement, you would trigger a guaranteed annual cash flow for life. The guarantee is the greatest of three levels: 1) what you would get from the Social Security system, 2) 4% of your balance annually compounded at 4% over your earning career when you were contributing, or most likely 3) 4% of your balance in the account on an annual basis in retirement (Goody #4). The third scenario is most likely for younger participants because they would have more time in the system. Current retires could also opt into the system for the healthcare benefits and get paid what they would otherwise receive from Social Security. For those who opt into the FAST during their working career, this cash flow goes on in perpetuity and your heirs are able to inherit it (Goody #5). Today when a Social Security recipient and his or her spouse dies, Social Security payments stop.

What would this mean for our hero, the single mom? Suppose she worked for over 40 years and never made more than $25,000 in her career. According to Social Security, she could expect to get $14,676 per year that would be potentially taxable and end at her death. Under scenario #2 above, at retirement she would have amassed an account balance of $381,837 that would yield an annual tax-free cash flow of at least $15,273 that would continue to her heirs in perpetuity. Under scenario #3 above, if you assume the historical 10.2% average annual market return, she would amass a retirement account of $1,134,042 that would yield at least

> *Participants in Plan For America will get to see their payroll taxes, that would otherwise never be seen again, placed into an account in their own name.*

$45,362 per year tax-free and continue on to her heirs.

Just to summarize so far, we have covered four of the five areas of financial planning: investments, taxes, retirement, and estate planning, or leaving a legacy for your heirs. Participants in Plan For America will get to see their payroll taxes, that many would otherwise never see again, placed in an account in their own name. Their contributions would be tax-deductible and they would enjoy the upside of market returns with a guaranteed minimum return, and enjoy a tax-free income stream in retirement for life that they can pass along to their heirs in perpetuity. Who would not sign up?

At this point, we might have to explain a little how the plan works because you are probably wondering: how can the trust guarantee a return? This is where the funding mechanism comes in. Every year the FAST charges 2% of the assets in the trust. Today the payroll taxes total about $1 trillion every year so if everyone signed up for Plan For America, the 2% the FAST would receive in the first year would be about $20 billion.

As discussed, the investments in the trust would be virtually costless to maintain, and the 2% fee has a very important role. These monies will be used to first, pay off current retirees. It would not be fair for those who have paid into the Social Security system their entire lives not to get a return. Once these obligations to those retirees are met, the 2% fee can then be used to retire government debt and ultimately become the sole funding source for government. How long this will take depends on market returns and how quickly Americans choose to enroll in the FAST and abandon the old system. Our estimate is, that all government unfunded liabilities will be gone somewhere between 2059-2079.

That all sounds great, but we are sure some of you are thinking that the market does not go up in a straight line. There are frequently down years (about one in every four), and some of those are very severe. How will that affect my FAST payments? We answer this in more detail in the "How it Works" portion of the book. The short answer is that when you retire, your first distribution is a minimum below which you cannot fall. If the first year after you retire is a down year in the market, the FAST will still pay you the minimum you have earned (4% of account balance compounded at 4%). If there is a severe market downturn and your account drops below a certain level, the FAST will automatically give you an interest-free loan against your account to keep your account at that level. In up market years, you automatically pay the FAST back out of the excess earnings in your account. These loans to keep guaranteed returns are also a use of the annual 2% fee charged by the FAST. Of course, in up years without a loan against your account, you receive more than the guaranteed minimum.

One other nagging question you might have is that, while $20 billion is a lot of money in the first year, that is nowhere near close to enough to pay off current Social Security recipients, even after several years of taking in a fee of that size, and that is absolutely true. Going back to the contract, one of the provisions is that the FAST can borrow money by issuing bonds and the federal government will guarantee these bonds and pay the interest on them.

Once the 2% annual fee grows large enough, the bonds will be retired and when that happens, all unfunded liabilities will be gone. We estimate the FAST will issue between $48-71 trillion of bonds, at the most, in order to pay off current retirees and dig us out of this debt hole. Depending on market returns, these

Getting out of our national debt will not happen overnight, but it is better than the current plan, which is not plan at all.

bonds will be retired between 2059-2079. When they are, all unfunded liabilities will be gone. While that is a lot of money, it is nowhere near the $100+ trillion in unfunded liabilities now, and those liabilities will decline as the FAST grows. Getting out of our national debt will not happen overnight, to be sure, but it is better than the current plan which is no plan at all.

Healthcare

We have explained the retirement portion of Plan For America but wait, there is more! As stated earlier, 12.4% of your payroll taxes go to Social Security and only 2.9% for Medicare, yet healthcare is the biggest driver of government debt by far. The other part of the Plan For America contract is that the federal government agrees to get out of the healthcare business (in addition to the retirement business) in exchange for being relieved of $100-200 trillion in unfunded liabilities.

Here is what the healthcare portion does: upon opting into the FAST for your own retirement account, you will be automatically eligible for a healthcare policy. This policy is uni-age, uni-sex, and guaranteed issue, meaning you cannot be turned down for coverage for any reason, including pre-existing conditions. Like Obamacare, your children can stay on your policy until age 26.

The policy comes with a standard premium of $11,200 per year that includes a $1,200 Health Savings Account (HSA). The policy comes with a $1 million cap in coverage (Goody #1), and you can spend it however you want on the healthcare of your choice (Goody #2). Again, it is YOUR insurance policy! Before recipients are eligible for Medicare, many private healthcare plans do not cover treatments such as chiropractic or acupuncture, for example, but you can spend your FAST healthcare dollars on

The HSA cost is designed to include all co-pays and deductibles so there are no out of pocket costs for physician visits or anything else in the course of a given year.

them if you want. Once in Medicare, it only covers a limited amount of nursing home care, for example, but the FAST covers it all, up to the $1 million cap.

22

The built-in HSA encourages preventive care. The $1,200 cost is designed to include all co-pays and deductibles so there are no out-of-pocket costs for physician visits or anything else in the course of a given year. At the end of the year, the unused portion of the HSA is returned to you tax-free (Goody #3). We believe this will encourage people not to be wasteful with their healthcare dollars.

To clarify, the $11,200 premium is per individual, not per household, so a married couple would pay $22,400 annually. We recognize that many could not afford this, so one provision of the plan is that if you earn less than $40,000 who file their taxes singly or $80,000 filing jointly, you are eligible for an interest-free loan against your retirement account to pay the entire premium each year(Goody #4). The principle here is that *no one pays for anyone else's healthcare.* There is a sliding income scale whereby those with incomes up to $70,000 filing singly/$140,000 filing jointly would be eligible for partial loans to help pay their premiums.

The FAST healthcare is truly universal in that it covers EVERY U.S. Citizen who signs up (Goody #5). No one can be denied coverage, even if you do not have a job. We believe the provisions of these policies will serve to keep health insurance costs down because of competition among insurance companies to offer their policies to American Citizens. All health insurance policies would be offered on a national instead of a state level.

To summarize for the healthcare portion, there will be universal coverage for every U.S. Citizen who signs up. Participants will have $1 million of lifetime coverage that can be spent however they want on their healthcare needs. Each plan comes with a Health Savings Account that covers all deductibles and co-pays for the year, and the unused portion is returned at the end of the year tax-free. And, for those unable to afford the premium, there is an interest-free loan against the retirement plan, making the policy affordable. What is not to like?

We are sure there are some practical questions you have without diving into the weeds of how the plan works and we will attempt to address those here. Some of you might be wondering if $1 million is enough for lifetime coverage, for starters. For some it will not be. In those cases, participants will have one of two choices. They can either buy more insurance on the open market out of pocket, or, if they cannot afford more coverage, they can get an interest-free loan against their retirement account for as long as necessary once the cap is reached after they have exhausted their own resources. In either case, no one pays for anyone else's healthcare and no one is denied the necessary healthcare because of money.

Others of you might be thinking, "I just want to get into the FAST for the retirement benefits. I do not want the healthcare." In that case, the participant can put $100,000 into an escrow account. If for some reason she then falls ill and needs coverage, this account is tapped to pay for it until the account is replenished. If it is not, she is automatically enrolled in the FAST healthcare. Again, no one pays for anyone else's healthcare!

The big question has to be, for those who cannot afford the healthcare premiums, what effect will borrowing against your retirement account have on the account if you "owe" tens or hundreds of thousands of dollars at the time of death? This goes back to the five areas of financial planning we discussed earlier. We have already addressed investing, taxation, retirement and estate planning. Now comes insurance.

Life Insurance

For those who do need an interest-free loan against their accounts, one provision of the FAST is that any loan automatically triggers a life insurance policy equal to the size of the loan. The premiums for this are built into the loan. At the time of death, let's say the individual owes $500,000 in lifetime healthcare premiums to his FAST account. During her working years, her retirement account grows and in retirement, she still gets a guaranteed annual payment. But because

> *For those who do need an interest-free loan against their retirement accounts to pay for the healthcare, one provision of the plan is that any loan automatically triggers a life insurance policy equal to the size of the loan.*

she has a loan against her account, she only gets the guaranteed minimum.

Going back to our hero, the single mom, let's see how this would specifically apply to her. Under the scenario that she amassed roughly $380,000 in her retirement account, she would be entitled to a minimum 5% payout in retirement because she had a loan against her account. This would give her about $19,000 per year in income in retirement. At the time of death, the life insurance would pay $120,000 into her account to equal the $500,000 loan.

Notice we did not say that the entire $500,000 is used to pay off the loan. We want the FAST to take its 2% fee on that $500,000 in perpetuity. Instead the annual payments that would otherwise go to heirs are used to pay off the loan over time. Once the loan is paid, the designated heirs start to receive the annual cash flow from the retirement account in perpetuity. Using life insurance in this way even allows healthcare coverage for an individual who never works a day in his life and would cover current retirees who never had a FAST account in their working years.

Ramifications

There are many ramifications from this plan that we feel will benefit our nation. First and foremost, adoption of the plan will shift our country from a culture of debt to one of equity. What we mean by that is that right now we are awash in debt, not just at the government level but at the corporate and consumer levels as well. Under Plan For America, our national savings rate will go up 15.3% overnight and American Citizens will be owners of corporate America through participation in the all-market index.

> *First and foremost, adoption of the plan will shift our country from a culture of debt to one of equity.*

We also believe that this plan will be a unifying force in our nation. Right now we are in a time of extreme partisan polarization, and this plan is designed to be non-partisan by appealing to ideas on all sides of the political spectrum. In a time when it is difficult to get the two major parties in our country to agree on anything, we think there are enough goodies in this plan to win over constituents on both sides of the aisle.

For example, Democrats and those on the left should like that the so-called Wall Street "fat cats" will be working for the ordinary citizen. In fact, the ordinary citizen will "own" Wall Street by virtue of their shares of stock in the index. Liberals will like that we have also built in provisions for good corporate governance and ways to ensure that corporate compensation for executives in the publicly traded companies do not get out of hand, and you can read more about that in the "How It Works" section.   Democrats will also appreciate a single-payer healthcare system, for which they have been advocating for quite a while.

Republicans and those on the right will like that the plan preserves the free-market capitalistic system that has generated such wealth for our nation over time.   Private healthcare is ensured, and they should also like the personal responsibility aspect that each individual is responsible for his or her healthcare.   Conservatives will like the fiscal responsibility and discipline that the plan will offer to get rid of all government debts and deficits.

Another ramification we did not specifically address in what the plan does is in relation to the states.   We covered that one major aspect of our debt problem in this nation is the unfunded pension liabilities for many of the states.   Remember that the states are signatories to the contract that establishes the FAST, and a big benefit for them is that their pensioners can be placed into the FAST with personal accounts just like any other individual.   This will allow the states to offload that burden and, once the FAST has retired all federal debts and deficits, the state and federal governments will both benefit from the increasing funding stream the 2% FAST fee will generate.

Perhaps the best way to summarize what Plan For America does is to imagine it through the eyes of our hero.   By participating in the FAST, she will have a tax-free income stream in retirement that she can pass on to her heirs and a healthcare plan she can spend on nursing home care if she needs it in retirement.   Best of all, she will know that she will be leaving a legacy to her heirs.

Summary of Chapter Three:

- Plan For America is unique because it has a funding mechanism, the benefits are better than current entitlement programs, it is established by contract law which is harder to change than legislation, and is aided by compounding interest.

- Participants get their own retirement accounts with tax-deductible contributions that enjoy the potential upside of market returns with a guaranteed minimum and have a tax-free income stream for life in retirement that passes on to heirs forever.

- The healthcare is universal for every Citizen with a $1 million lifetime cap that can be spent on whatever kind of care you want; each plan has an HSA covering all deductibles and co-pays with the unused portion returned tax-free at year end; those who cannot afford premiums get interest-free loans against their retirement accounts covered by life insurance.

Chapter 4

What Can You Do to Help?

Now that you know about the plan, what can you do to help? Something of this size and complexity will not be easy to get enacted. In fact, about the only objection that others raise when we share this plan with them is that it will be too difficult to get enacted politically because it is such a big idea and covers so many areas. That does not worry us because, when it comes down to it, politicians will fold when they feel enough pressure from the electorate.

We remember one story we were told by a sitting congressman about correspondence he receives. He said if he received a hand-written letter on a particular issue, it got his attention. If he received 3-5 such letters, he would consider changing his position. And if he received 10 letters like that, he would be afraid of being recalled! In other words, he knew how many people just one letter represents and he was talking about personalized letters, not mass-produced postcards. We are not ready for you to contact your congressman or woman yet, but the following three steps are things we ask that you do now:

1. **Like us on Facebook**.

We have created a Facebook page and it has over 50,000 followers so far. This is a nice start, but we will need hundreds of thousands, and perhaps millions, to get the attention of those in office and elsewhere. It is also an efficient way for us to get news out about what we are doing and the progress that is being made on the plan.

2. **Share your contact information with us.**

We do not own the Facebook platform, so as we decide to use other communication vehicles, it will be helpful to have your contact so that we can keep in touch with you. Your name and an email address or cell phone number is all that we need and you can send that to us at eric@planforamerica.us. We welcome your thoughts and ideas on the plan as well.

3. **Give!**

Plan For America is a 501(c)(3) non-profit organization. All contributions are tax-deductible and you can contribute through our website at www.planforamerica.us. So far this project has been funded out of our own pockets and we need more resources to be able to get the word out. This book is one part of that process. When you give, depending upon the level, we will send a small gift as a token of our appreciation such as a Plan For American pin or hat. Any amount will help!

One thing we want you to know is that we are all in this together. This plan was designed with the American people in mind. In fact, if anything, this plan might hurt our business if it is adopted! We are investment advisors, and if most Americans have FAST accounts instead of 401k plans for their retirements, there will be less money for us to manage in the form of rollover IRAs.

We appeal to you as fellow patriots to help keep this country on a sound financial footing. If that is lost, it could mean dark days for all of us. We will spell out what a failure to solve our debt and deficit problems might look like in the next chapter.

Summary of Chapter Four:

- **There are many ways you can help**
- **Like us on Facebok**
- **Give us your contact info**
- **Make a tax-deductible donation to:**

www.PlanForAmerica.us

Chapter 5

Avoiding Failure: National Bankruptcy

There are only three ways to address debt: 1) pay it off, 2) roll it over, or 3) repudiate it. Some of the questions you might have are, "why do we even have to pay it off at all? Doesn't our central bank, the Federal Reserve, have what is called a "magic checkbook" that can make any financial obligation disappear? And do we not just owe the money to ourselves, so it doesn't make any difference anyway?"

There are some who believe this, but the laws of economics are very unforgiving when it comes to debts. They must be paid off or others will lose confidence in the debtor, and it must be remembered that our entire financial system works on confidence. If confidence is ever lost in the system to the point that no one is willing to take the dollar as payment, we have entered *national bankruptcy*.

> *If confidence is ever lost in the system to the point that no one is willing to take the dollar as payment, we have entered national bankruptcy.*

The first option, to pay off the debt, is not possible on our current path. The U.S. government does not generate any surplus revenues, and has not for the past 20 years, let alone enough surplus to start paying down the debt. If the government tried to print enough money to pay it off, it would make the dollar worthless. Remember that scarcity generally makes something more valuable, while a glut makes it less so. Germany experienced hyper-inflation following World War I and there are stories of citizens there taking wheelbarrows full of cash to the local bakery to buy a loaf of bread.

The next option, rolling over the debt, is what we have been doing for decades. Another term for this is "kicking the can down the road." In order to finance this, the government issues bonds. Right now the interest payments on those bonds is modest because prevailing interest rates are low, but what happens when interest rates start to rise again? When they do, interest on the debt will consume an increasing portion of our federal budget and will squeeze out the ability to pay for basic services like our entitlement programs. Our debts cannot be rolled over forever.

Repudiating debt, or refusing to pay it, is a tactic only tried by lesser developed countries. By not paying debt, those hurt are the ones to whom the debt is owed, and those people are current and future U.S. Citizens. Just like when a Ponzi scheme comes to its bitter end, at the point of debt repudiation, those Americans who

What would a bankrupt America look like?

have paid into the system their entire lives will be told there is nothing left for them.

What would a bankrupt America look like? In a word, scary. Aside from law enforcement issues, let's just consider it from a social programs perspective. There would be no Social Security so citizens would have to work until they died or were physically incapable of doing so. Only the wealthy could afford to retire, and even their standard of living would take a tremendous hit in a bankrupt America.

Likewise, there would be no Medicare or Medicaid and therefore no secure healthcare. Only those who could afford a private doctor would get care. But it does not have to be like this. There is another way and it is not too late. In the next chapter we will take a high level view of what success would look like.

Summary of Chapter Five:

- **If nothing changes, we are on the road to national bankruptcy**

- **Bankruptcy means no secure retirement**

- **Bankruptcy mean no secure healthcare.**

Chapter 6

Achieving Success: the Best Social Safety Net in the World

Let's suppose Plan For America is adopted. Our entitlement programs would be enhanced and placed on a secure foundation forever. There would actually be a mechanism to pay down the debt, the 2% fee taken by the FAST of all assets in the trust, and the government would not have to print one extra dollar to do so. Of course, it will take some time because we have dug ourselves quite a deep hole of debt, but finally there would be hope it will happen.

American Citizens will then stop worrying about their futures. Questions like, "Will I have enough to live on in retirement?" and "Will I have the quality of healthcare I need later in life?" will be greatly reduced. In fact, U.S. Citizenship, already of tremendous

Instead of future generations being burdened by debt, they will be relieved by revenue streams generated on their behalf before they are even born.

value, will become the gold standard of the world because we will have the greatest social safety net anywhere in the world.

In retirement, Americans will be able to draw 4% of their retirement account balance, tax-free, every year, and have a guaranteed minimum payment in down market years. In up market years, they will realize the full benefit and not be capped on how much they can make. The ever-growing cash flow is inheritable, tax-free in perpetuity so instead of future generations being burdened by debt, they will be relieved by revenue streams generated on their behalf before they are even born.

Every American will have affordable, high quality healthcare for life. In fact, a single citizen who never earns more than $40,000 will have free healthcare for life because he or she will be eligible for interest-free loans against the retirement account. And the healthcare dollars can be spent on whatever form of care the individual chooses.

From a corporate standpoint, companies will be able to rely on a steady stream of accessible cash by issuing stock if they are part of the FAST all-market index. This will allow citizens to be owners of corporate America and it will allow corporations to retire their bonds and

Imagine no taxes of any kind: no income tax, no sales tax, no capital gains tax, no estate tax!

shift to equity, or stock, funding. Companies from all over the world will be looking to relocate to America to be part of this index. All of this economic activity will be good for the markets and for employment.

Once all the debts are retired, the 2% funding mechanism will become the sole revenue source for state and federal governments. Imagine no taxes of any kind: no income tax, no sales tax, no capital gains tax, no estate tax! While this heavenly ideal is still a way down the road, it is not too early to dream. It has been said that "a rising tide lifts all boats" and what we are proposing with Plan For America is a massive rising tide.

If you are convinced that Plan For America is the answer to our nation's debt problems, you can stop reading this book right now. If you still have questions or want to know how the plan actually works, keep reading Parts II and III and your questions should be answered. If you still have a question after all of that, please contact us at terry@planforamerica.us.

Summary of Chapter Six:

- **Under Plan For America, we will have the greatest social safety net in the world.**

- **There will be secure retirement and healthcare benefit with better benefits than we enjoy today.**

- **Ultimately, there will be no need for taxation of any kind.**

The 'Plan For America'

How to Place the American Dream on a Sure Foundation Forever

Part II

How Plan For America Works

www.PlanForAmerica.us

Chapter 7

Key Questions

Now that you know what Plan For America does, this part will explain how it works. It follows a Question & Answer format, and the questions are numbered for easy reference. This section of the book is divided into five chapters by topic, so you can go to the chapters and questions that interest you the most. If you think of a question that we have not covered, please ask us!

1. Why is a contract needed to protect the interests of "We the People?"

We need a contract to protect us from changes in government.

The government has the power to pass laws and repeal them. If we put a plan in place that solves America's retirement, healthcare, and debt funding problems, we must protect it with a contract. Otherwise, a future government could repeal the whole plan.

A contract is a legal agreement that has penalties for violating the terms of what each side has promised to live up to. A contract will be long-lasting if it is of benefit to everyone concerned. Let's look at the three parties involved:

1. We the People, represented by the For America Security Trust (FAST)

2. The Federal Government, represented by Uncle Sam

3. The 50 States, represented by The Statesman

We the People

Benefits: what We the People get out of the deal

- America will have a retirement and health care trust (FAST) that is independently funded, not depending on the government or the politicians.
- America's retirement and health care benefits will be secure and fully funded rather than heading toward collapse and bankruptcy.
- Retirement and disability benefits are guaranteed to be at least equal to what Social Security presently provides, but in most cases will be far greater.
- Healthcare benefits will be comprehensive and far greater for every U.S. citizen than what is being offered under Medicare, Medicaid or Obamacare.
- Pre-existing conditions will be covered as well as there being no ultimate cap on the amount of health care benefits that will be paid. Also, children can remain on their parents' health insurance plans until reaching age 26.
- No government health panels — all health care decisions will be made by the doctor and the patient.
- All health insurance policies will be individually owned and can be obtained and used anywhere in the United States.
- Healthcare will be truly affordable and interest-free loans will be available to those with lower incomes. The interest-free loans do not have to be paid back with out-of-pocket funds; they can be repaid from the excess returns on the individual's FAST account.

- Under the Standard Plan offered through the FAST, the $1200 annual Health Savings Account would equal the maximum total of the deductible plus the co-pay so that there would be no out-of-pocket healthcare cost other than the premium.
- Under the Plan For America, no one (meaning the taxpayers) would have to pay for anyone else's healthcare.
- There are numerous tax savings for almost every working American.
- All retirement benefits paid by the FAST will be 100% tax-free and when the benefits pass to the heirs, they will be estate tax and income tax-free.
- All insurance benefits — health, life, and disability- will be tax-free and any of the Health Savings Account that is not used on deductibles or co-pays can be withdrawn tax-free at the end of the year.
- All FAST retirement contributions and insurance premiums will be 100% tax-deductible on a federal and state basis.
- Each year over $1 trillion will be injected into the U.S. capital markets — millions of jobs should be created on an ongoing basis.
- The Millennials and Gen Z (those born after 1980) can be confident that the money that they are paying in (15.3% of earnings) for their retirement and future healthcare will be there for them in their own account, unlike now where their payroll taxes are only going to support the older generations. These generations realize that Social Security and Medicare will not be around by the time they need it.
- The 15.3% contributions enjoy the *best* of both worlds — that is, stock market returns with a 4% minimum guarantee for growth and safety that is backed by the "full faith and credit" of the U.S. Government.

- The Plan For America will make a basic financial plan available to every U.S. citizen, even those with very low income. This financial plan would include: health insurance, disability insurance, life insurance, retirement benefits, tax benefits, and an estate legacy for even the lowest income wage earner.

Costs: What do We the People have to give up?

Zero — Nada — Nothing!

We the People's reaction to the deal —

What is not to like? All pluses and no minuses, massive job creation, a federal government moving toward fiscal responsibility instead of bankruptcy, tax reduction, secure and increased retirement and health care benefits, and no longer having to live in fear that everything is going to collapse in financial ruin. Give us the contract, we'll gladly sign!

Uncle Sam

Benefits: what Uncle Sam gets out of the deal

- Being relieved of an estimated $120 trillion of what are called unfunded liabilities — this is the amount of money that will be needed to pay for all of the promised benefits from Social Security and Medicare.
- Being relieved of the yearly Federal Medicaid costs — it is estimated that the Federal Government spent $406 billion in 2019 on Medicaid (see https://ccf.georgetown.edu/2019/02/28/medicaid-and-state-budgets-checking-the-facts-yet-again/). According to the Centers for Medicare and Medicaid Service, Medicaid is expected to grow at 5.4% each year. At that rate it will reach $557 billion by 2025!

- Between 2059 and 2079, the FAST will have paid off all of the unfunded liabilities and will give the Federal Government 50% of its yearly surplus which is expected to be trillions of dollars each year to pay off the national debt.
- After the national debt has been fully repaid, the 50% of the annual surplus trillions from the FAST would be used to reduce taxation and eventually become the main funding source for Federal Government operations, replacing the need for taxation.

Costs: what does Uncle Sam have to contribute to the deal?

- The Federal Government must allow any and all citizens that want to opt out of Social Security, Medicare, Medicaid and Obamacare and join the FAST to do so.
- The U.S. Government must get out of the retirement and healthcare providing businesses (with the exception of those not opting out of Social Security, Medicare, Medicaid, and Obamacare).
- The U.S. Government will not take equity in private enterprise.
- Repeal the payroll taxes for all who join the FAST.
- Make all contributions to the FAST tax-deductible. The present level of the payroll tax is calculated on earnings up to $137,700. At the option of the one contributing, if he/she has earnings over $137,700, the tax-deductible contribution could be increased to 15.3% of total earnings.
- In addition to the 15.3% of earnings contribution, each member of the FAST could contribute up to $100,000 annually and be fully tax-deductible.
- Since the FAST is assuming the responsibility, redirect the interest payments on the non-negotiable notes held by the Social Security and Medicare Trust Funds to

the FAST. Ultimately, the FAST will pay off these notes as well.

• All premiums for health, disability and life insurance as well as the health savings account purchased through the FAST would be 100% tax-deductible.

• All retirement payouts and insurance benefit payouts would be 100% income tax-free.

• Any portion of the health savings account left over at the end of the year (not used for deductibles or co-pays) can be withdrawn tax-free.

• The annual retirement payouts upon the death of the one who made the contributions would pass income tax-free and estate tax-free to the heirs.

• All ordinary (cash) dividends on common stock of publicly-held, U.S. domiciled corporations would be tax-deductible to the corporation and tax-free to the one who receives the dividend.

• The FAST would issue bonds to pay for the present Social Security retirement and disability benefits and the interest-free loans made to those who could not afford their health insurance premiums. The U.S. Government would pay the interest on these bonds and guarantee them with the "full faith and credit" of the U.S. Government.

• The FAST would call in and pay off the principal on the bonds out of its growing annual revenues.

Uncle Sam's reaction to the deal —

WOW! What a deal! Where do I sign? This is better than buying Manhattan Island for $24, or buying the state of Alaska from the Russians for $7.2 million! I get to escape the consequences for the sins that the politicians have committed through the years. Yahoo!

The Statesman

Benefits: What does The Statesman get out of the deal?

- Each state would be relieved of most of its Medicaid obligations (except for the small number of people that may not choose to join the FAST) which makes up about 17% of its total budget.
- Each state (if it elects to do so) could be relieved of its pension liabilities — both the funded and unfunded portions.
- Between 2059 and 2079, the FAST will have paid off all of the unfunded liabilities and give each of the states its share of 50% of the FAST's annual surplus, which is expected to be trillions of dollars each year to pay off the states' debts. The pro rata share for each individual state will be determined by the percentage of national GDP that is generated in that state.
- After the state's debt has been fully repaid, then the 50% of annual surplus trillions from the FAST would be used to reduce taxation and eventually become the main funding source for each state's government operations, replacing the need for taxation.

Costs: what does The Statesman have to contribute to the deal?

- The loss of tax revenues (for states that have an income tax) on the FAST contributions representing 7.65% of earned income up to the current $137,700 cap.
- The loss of tax revenues (for states that have an income tax) on the FAST contributions over the $137,700 cap if the FAST participant elects to contribute beyond the cap. This could represent 15.3% of the total earnings above the cap.

- The loss of tax revenue on the elective contribution (for states that have an income tax) of up to $100,000 annually for each FAST member that elects to participate — regardless of his/her earnings.
- Each state's tax-free municipal bonds would have to compete with the tax-free dividends from U.S. domiciled publicly-held corporations. This would likely require that these bonds pay higher rates of interest in order to attract investors.

The Statesman's reaction to the deal —

This is a great deal! Where do I sign? The Medicaid costs and the unfunded liabilities have put some of our states in danger of bankruptcy. This deal offers us a painless way out. Count me in!

2. What are the terms of the contract between the For America Security Trust (FAST) and the individual participants?

The FAST commits to provide the following to the individual participants:

To take in all participant contributions and invest the money into an all U.S. equities (stock) fund similar to a total market index fund.

To provide a guarantee of a compounded 4% rate of return on all participant investment accounts, and, upon retirement, pay out a minimum 4% of that amount annually.

To provide the stock market's actual annual return less 2% for the FAST charge for delivering:

- the administration of the plan,

- the 4% guarantee,
- interest-free loans to FAST accounts to protect against "drawdown" during times when the stock market is under severe pressure,
- interest-free loans for those who cannot afford the premiums for their health insurance,
- and a guarantee that retirement and disability benefits will be at least the level that they are under Social Security.

To provide access to insurance companies that offer high-quality, comprehensive health insurance to all FAST participants.

- Pre-existing conditions will be covered at standard rates.
- There will be no ultimate cap on the amount of benefits that will be provided.
- All health care decisions will be made by the doctor and the patient — no government panels.
- All health insurance policies will be individually owned and can be obtained and used anywhere in the United States.
- The "standard" health insurance plan would include a $1,200 annual health savings account. The maximum total amount of the co-pay plus the deductible would = $1,200; therefore, the only out-of-pocket cost would be the premium for the insurance. If any of the $1,200 in the health savings account is not consumed by the end of the year, then any amount left over can be withdrawn tax-free.
- Guaranteed insurability for life and disability insurance is provided as part of the "standard" plan.
- Interest-free loans will be available to those who cannot afford the insurance premiums. These interest-free loans do not have to be repaid with out-of-pocket

funds; they can be repaid from the excess returns on the individual's FAST account.

To provide tax benefits to the participants through the terms of the contract that the FAST would have with the Federal Government and the 50 States.

- All retirement contributions made by the participants will be 100% tax-deductible.
- All insurance premiums paid to the FAST will be 100% tax-deductible.
- All benefits, retirement or insurance will be 100% tax-free to the participants when paid out.
- Under the Plan For America, no one, meaning the taxpayers, would have to pay for anyone else's health care.
- Under this Plan For America, all retirement benefits (the annual cash flow) will be paid to the heirs upon the death of the participant with no income or estate taxation.

What do the participants have to do to comply with our part of the contract?

- First, you have to opt out (withdraw) from Social Security, Medicare, Medicaid and Obamacare and join the FAST.
- Second, the 15.3% that is the amount of the current payroll taxes will be withheld from your paycheck through a payroll reduction agreement and sent to your account in the FAST.
- Third, you must enroll in a health insurance plan through the FAST, unless you qualify to opt out. Remember, under Plan For America (PFA), no one, meaning the taxpayers, would have to pay for anyone else's health care.

3. *Why would Plan For America appeal to liberal Americans?*

Plan For America would appeal to liberal Americans for the following reasons:

- PFA provides for comprehensive healthcare insurance for every U.S. citizen with no pre-existing condition exclusion and no ultimate cap on the benefits.
- Children could remain on their parent's or guardian's plan until reaching age 26.
- The ultimate funding guarantee for PFA is the "full faith and credit" of the U.S. Government as are the present social programs — Social Security, Medicare, Medicaid and Obamacare.
- The retirement age would not be raised in fact retirement could begin as early as age 60 at the worker's option.
- Retirement benefits would not be reduced regardless of how much the retired worker earned in retirement.
- Pension benefits for public employee unions could be protected.
- Executive compensation would be under close scrutiny which would have a limiting effect on very high pay without corresponding outstanding results.
- PFA's funding approach would make retirement and health care benefits much more secure than the precarious funding scheme that is presently in effect.
- There would be a "single payer" for health, disability and life insurance premiums. PFA makes the premium payments through payroll reduction and provides interest-free loans for those who have lost their jobs or cannot afford the premiums.
- A great degree of "Social" and "Economic" Justice" would be achieved under PFA because the

retirement plan of the workers and retirees will ultimately own the greatest part of U.S. corporations.

- Under PFA wealth distribution will be much more equitable.
- PFA would end the regressive payroll tax.
- Every worker, even moderate and low-income wage earners would have a legacy to pass on to his/her heirs.
- PFA provides for a financial plan for moderate and low-income American workers including disability and life insurance on a guaranteed-issue basis.
- The benefits from Wall Street will flow primarily to the retirement plan of the workers and retirees instead of to the "Fat Cats."

4. Why would Plan For America (PFA) appeal to conservative and libertarian Americans?

Plan For America would appeal to conservative and libertarian Americans for the following reasons:

- PFA incorporates tax reduction as part of the strategy. The payroll tax is eliminated, corporate dividends become tax-free as well as being tax-deductible to the corporation, and the retirement benefit cash flow is income tax-free and estate tax-free when it passes to the participant's heirs.
- PFA retirement account will be held by an independent trust, not by the government as is Social Security.
- Healthcare for all U.S. citizens under PFA is provided through individual health insurance policies, not government provided or controlled.
- Participation in PFA is voluntary; joining the For America Security Trust (FAST) enables individuals to

opt out of Social Security, Medicare, Medicaid, and Obamacare.

• Under PFA, each individual will ultimately pay for his/her own retirement, health care insurance, disability insurance, and life insurance.

• PFA contract with the federal and state governments requires the U.S. Government to get out of the retirement and health care businesses as well as any and all aspects of private enterprise.

• Each participant and his/her heirs get to keep the wealth that they have contributed via perpetual cash flow.

• The federal and state governments should be able to balance their budgets in a very short period of time because under PFA the burden of the major entitlement programs would be eliminated.

• PFA provides the funding method to pay off federal and state debt.

• PFA will ultimately provide the funds to eliminate the need for taxation at the federal and state levels.

• The size of the federal and state governments should shrink under PFA because government services would not be needed in many areas.

5. How reasonable is the 2% charge from the For America Security Trust (FAST) for what it provides, and is it a good investment for "We the People?"

For what the FAST provides, a 2% charge is extremely reasonable and it is an excellent investment. The following are the benefits for the FAST participant:

• All contributions to the FAST are 100% tax-deductible.
• All growth of the invested assets is 100% tax-free.
• All payouts from the FAST are 100% tax-free.

- All payouts to heirs after the death of the participant are 100% income and estate tax-free.
- All contributions (for the purposes of retirement payouts) are guaranteed to have a minimum 4% compounded annual rate of return and to payout 4% of that amount.
- All contributions will receive each year's market rate of return on the FAST stock portfolio less 2% for its charge.
- The FAST will provide an interest-free loan to the participant's account if the market is suffering a downturn and the participant's account is in danger of experiencing "drawdown."
- The FAST will provide interest-free loans to participants that cannot afford their health care insurance premiums or for those who have exceeded the maximum benefit on their health care insurance and cannot afford to pay for the medical costs.
- The greatest benefit of all is saving the United States from financial disaster and bankruptcy, where all benefits and government services would be lost.

Contributions to the FAST are an excellent investment. Any investor would love to have the opportunity to have an investment that:

- Is tax-deductible and pays out tax-free.
- Passes to heirs' estate tax-free.
- Is guaranteed by the "full faith and credit" of the U.S. Government.
- Guarantees a 4% rate of return.
- Earns the stock market returns less 2%.
- Provides interest-free loans for health care needs.

6. What actions could be taken to initiate Plan For America (PFA)?

One way to initiate Plan For America could be:

- Have Congress pass a bill and signed by the President into law authorizing the Federal Court to appoint a Receiver for the For America Security Trust (FAST).
- The Receiver would have the authority to appoint five interim trustees to operate the FAST until the votes can be taken for the initial five elected trustees.
- The Receiver would have the authority to tap a line of credit extended from the U.S. Government to the Receiver for the purposes of establishing the FAST and enabling it to become operational.
- This line of credit would be repaid along with all costs for the Receivership upon the first bond offering by the FAST, which should occur shortly after becoming operational.
- A court-appointed Receivership would provide transparency because the court would require full reporting.
- A court-appointed Receivership would provide accountability because the court would require the Receiver to account fully for every penny.
- A court-appointed Receivership would provide safety because neither the politicians nor any unscrupulous individuals would have access to any of the funds.
- Any vendor contracts entered into by the court-appointed Receiver or the succeeding FAST Board of Trustees would have to be competitively bid and published for transparency along with a report outlining the rationale for granting the contract to that particular vendor.

Chapter 8

Retirement

1. How does the powerful funding method of the Plan For America work?

To begin, we must first establish the basic facts:

According to the Center on Budget and Policy Priorities, the total amount of payroll taxes (15.3% of earnings — 7.65% from the employee and 7.65% from the employer) was $1.24 trillion in 2019. Also in 2019, the interest payments from the U.S. Government for the $2.897 trillion that it owes to the Social Security and Medicare Trust Funds was $81 billion (see https://www.ssa.gov/policy/trust-funds-summary.html). The total cashflow to the FAST for 2019 would have been the sum of these two numbers, or $1.321 trillion.

The For America Security Trust (FAST) will be sent the entire 15.3% ($1.24 trillion if it was 2019) from each employer or self-employed individual throughout the year via payroll reduction -very similar to the payroll tax and exactly the same amount along with the annual interest payment due from the Federal Government on the Trust funds.

The FAST will set up an account for each contributor and credit the account with 100% of the contribution and then deduct 2% of that amount for the annual FAST charge.

The 2% charge is the only source of funding for the FAST to cover all of its operating expenses as well as providing a 4% minimum guaranteed return to the contributors. However, this funding method is extremely powerful. For example:

- 2% of $1 trillion is $20 billion.
- After two years, there would be an additional $1 trillion which would make the annual charge $40 billion.
- After three years, there would be an additional $1 trillion, the charge would have grown to $60 billion, etc.

This funding stream will grow to the $1 trillion annual mark and beyond. It is the source of money to retire all debt taken on for the funding of the unfunded liabilities as well as the monies necessary to retire all federal and state debt. It will also supply the revenues to ultimately reduce taxation on both the federal and state levels.

2. Under the Plan For America, how will money (15.3% of income) contributed to the For America Trust Fund (FAST) be invested?

The payroll contributions received by the FAST will be placed into a collection of U.S. corporate stocks (large, medium, and small companies) similar to a total market index. With an index-type approach, the cost of administering will be minimized since there will be no cost incurred for investment managers.

Historically, the U.S. stock market has returned about 10.2% compounded from 1926 through 2019 (according to Ibbotson Associates — a highly regarded source of statistical information on financial markets). Remember, this time period includes the Great Depression, World War II, the high inflation of the 1970's, the market crash of 2000 to 2002, and the most recent 2008 to 2009 "Great Recession."

The FAST guarantees at least a 4% compounded rate of return on all invested contributions for the purpose of retirement payouts. The FAST will charge each participant account 2% each year for administering the plan and for providing the guaranteed 4% compounded rate of return.

The amount credited to each participant's account will be the beginning of the year balance, plus any contributions, less any payouts for retirement or disability, multiplied by the market's return for that year (whether it be positive or negative) minus 2% for the FAST charge.

3. Why would employers pay the 7.65% that is being paid as their share of the current payroll taxes to the employees if the employees enrolled in the For America Security Trust (FAST) and payroll taxes were no longer required?

The employers' would in almost all cases increase the employees' pay by the 7.65% that they would save by not having to pay the payroll taxes because:

- If an employee did not opt into the FAST and out of Social Security and Medicare, then the employer would still have to pay the government the 7.65%.
- The employee would have his/her own health care insurance through the FAST, thus the employer would not have to provide it.
- There would be a great deal of publicity, and the employees would know that the employer was keeping the 7.65% which would strain relations with the workers.
- Implementation of the FAST would bring on a $1 trillion capital infusion every year to the economy which would be great for business. Almost all employers would

do whatever they could to encourage this economic activity.

• Employment levels would very likely increase greatly, and there would be more competition for workers. Consequently, employers would be prone to do whatever they could to retain their employees.

4. Is it necessary for the stock market to have 10% returns in order for the Plan For America to work?

The answer is no. If the stock market averages 6%-7% over the longer term, the PFA will work. That means the stock market can average 30–40% less than the longer-term 10.2% average and still be effective; but there can be no doubt that higher returns will make the results even better.

5. Are United States citizens required to join the For America Security (FAST)?

The answer is no. Each U.S. citizen gets to choose whether he/she wants to stay in the Social Security, Medicare, Medicaid, and Obamacare programs or opt out of them and into the

FAST plan. If it was required to join the FAST, then it would probably be a constitutional question under the "Commerce Clause."

Although it is not mandatory, most likely almost everyone will join the FAST because:

• The health care benefits are far greater.
• The retirement benefits are far greater.
• The tax benefits are greater.
• The benefits are more secure.
• The economy will be stronger, and more jobs will be created.

6. Is the For America Security Trust (FAST) plan guaranteed by the U.S. Government as are Social Security, Medicare, Medicaid, and Obamacare?

Ultimately, yes.

- The existing federal guarantee for Social Security and the health care programs is what is called the "full faith and credit" of the U.S. Government- that is, the U.S. Government's ability to borrow money.
- The so-called trust funds for Social Security and Medicare do not provide any security because the politicians have taken all of the money out of them and put in notes (which are IOU's of the Federal Government). The problem with these notes is the fact that the
- U.S. Government is $23 trillion in debt and is running annual deficits of over $1 trillion. Therefore, in order for the government to get money out of the trusts, the government would have to redeem the notes but it has no money and the only way to get the money is to borrow more.
- The U.S. Government backing for the FAST under the Plan for America in accord with the contract is to guarantee the FAST bonds with the "full faith and credit" of the U.S. Government.
- As you can plainly see, the government-guarantees in both cases are the same; it is the ability of the U.S. Government to borrow money.

This is not to say that the Plan For America with its FAST is just as risky and likely to fail as are Social Security, Medicare, Medicaid, and Obamacare.

- Remember, the annual 2% of FAST assets that represents an annual cash flow that is increasing by over

$20 billion each year is the means by which the FAST will pay off all of the bonds (debt) that it will incur from taking over the government's unfunded liabilities. *Therefore, it is unlikely that the FAST will ever have to rely on the federal guarantee or government's ability to borrow to pay off the FAST bonds.*

- The Federal Government, on the other hand, has no such growing cash flow source and is, therefore, very likely to continue to borrow ever greater amounts of money until its borrowing capacity is gone.

7. How are the retirement benefits calculated under the Plan For America, and how do they compare to the benefits under Social Security?

The PFA guarantees that each year's retirement benefit will be the greatest of the following three options; therefore, it will be at least equal to Social Security and most likely will be far greater.

- Option 1 — The present level of Social Security retirement benefits calculated for the participating individual.
- Option 2 — 4% of the total of all contributions made to the *For America Security Trust* (FAST) with a 4% compounded annual rate of return.
- Option 3 — 4% of the amount of the participating individual's FAST balance at the end of the previous year.

Now, let's look at some numbers:

Example 1: A 26-year old works for 41 years at $25,000 per year, never gets a raise, retires at 67 years of age, and has not needed loans to pay for health insurance premiums. (Source: calculator on Social Security website, https://www.ssa.gov)

Option 1 — Social Security annual retirement is expected to be $1,223 per month or $14,676 per year subject to annual cost of living increases.

Option 2 — 4% of all contributions made to the participating individual's FAST account along with a 4% compounded annual rate of return.

- Annual earnings $25,000 multiplied by 15.3% = $3,825 annual contribution ($3,825 X 4% compounded over 41 years= $381,837).
- 4% X $381,837 = $15,273 annually or $1,273 per month is the guaranteed minimum subject to annual market return increases.

Option 3 — 4% of the amount of the individual's FAST balance. 4% of all contributions made plus the average market rate of return over the last 94 years or 10.2% annually and subtracting the FAST charge of 2% to arrive at a net 8.2% compounded.

- Annual earnings $25,000 multiplied by 15.3% = $3,825 annual contribution ($3,825 X 8.2% compounded over 41 years = $1,134,042).
- 4% X $1,134,042 = $45,362 or $3,786 per month becomes the guaranteed minimum because it was the value when retirement was elected. Also, it was the highest value of the three options, therefore, it is the payout for that year.

Example 2: Same as above except the participant needs an interest-free loan to pay for her health insurance premiums.

Option 1 same as above

Option 2 same as above *except:*

- The cumulative interest-free loans that would require the excess earnings (over the 4% guarantee) would go to repay the FAST for the health insurance loans. This would prevent earnings increases for retirement.
- It is possible, although unlikely, that the Social Security matching guarantee would trigger an increase.
- Therefore, whenever the retiring participant's FAST account has under-performed the FAST portfolio (net of the 2% charge) by 2% or more, then the payout for that participant would be 5% of his/her balance rather than the normal 4%.
- See example on website of the 26-year old woman in the section entitled "What does **Plan For America** do for you?" Her annual payout on retirement would be $19,092 instead of $15,273 as shown in Option 2

Option 3 same as above *except* excess earnings over 4% would be used to repay the loan.

8.How does the For America Security Trust (FAST) determine investment return on participant contributions?

The FAST places all investments into a portfolio of only U.S. corporate stocks made up of large, medium and small companies similar to what is called a "total market index."

The amount credited to each participant's account will be the total return of the FAST investment portfolio minus 2% for the FAST charge and then multiplied by the individual participant's percentage of the total FAST account.

Historically the U.S. stock market has averaged about 10.2% compounded annually from 1926 through 2019.

For retirement income purposes, the FAST guarantees a 4% compounded annual rate of return on each participant's account.

9.What is "draw-down" and how is my For America Security Trust (FAST) account protected against this happening to my account?

"Draw-down" is something that can happen to a retirement account if it is invested in the stock market and there is an extended period of terrible market conditions similar to what occurred during the Great Depression of the 1930's.

If the account is paying out 4% of the guaranteed amount (as the FAST does) and the account keeps going down year after year, then the point will be reached when the account

value would be too low to recover and the payout would stop. The account would have lost all of its value and could no longer pay out any amount.

To protect the FAST accounts from "drawdown," there is a provision in the Plan For America that calls for an interest-free loan to be extended by the FAST to any account that falls below 60% of the guaranteed value for determining the payout. The loan is repaid in years of positive market returns that result in the account growing beyond the 60% mark. The 60% was chosen as the threshold because 6% (4% for the guaranteed payout and 2% for the FAST charge) is the minimum required and 6 is 10% of 60. Therefore, 10% is the maximum that could be drawn on the account in any year that it was down to the 60% minimum. The importance of this is the fact that the account base will never be put into a position that it could not recover from.

10. Why would an economic downturn likely be much less severe if the Plan For America was in effect?

First, the vast majority of all health insurance premiums would be paid through the For American Security Trust (FAST). Even if people lost their jobs, they would not lose their health insurance because of the interest-free loans available to them. The health care industry is about 1/6 of the U.S. economy and would not be greatly affected by an economic downturn because people's health insurance would remain intact.

Second, retirees would still receive their payouts each month even if there was a stock market decline. Although the payouts might be reduced, they would never go below the minimum guaranteed. In most cases, the payouts would be far greater than social security; accordingly, retirees would not be facing financial ruin. The cash flows from the retiree monthly payments going into the economy would also limit the severity of an economic downturn.

Third, the FAST contributions from all of the working contributors would likely be in excess of $1 trillion per year. The interest-free loans from the FAST to the accounts that fell below the 60% "draw-down" level *(see Question 9)* will all be used to purchase shares in the stock market index. This would help to keep the stock market from going into a serious decline.

11. Will more money be taken out of my paycheck under the Plan For America (PFA) than is taken now for Social Security and Medicare?

The answer is NO. Under each program, a total of 15.3% of your earned income is contributed. Presently, under the Social Security/Medicare plan, one half of the 15.3% (7.65%) is paid by you and the other half (7.65%) is paid by your employer.

Under the PFA, the same 15.3% would be contributed to your For America Security Trust (FAST) account, but the contributions would be tax-deductible for you. You most likely will end up with more money in your pocket from tax savings, depending upon your tax bracket.

Currently, your contribution to Social Security/Medicare is not tax-deductible. Participation in the FAST plan will provide more after-tax money for you each year because your contributions ARE tax-deductible.

12. If my contributions to the For America Security Trust (FAST) are tax-deductible, then will I have to pay taxes on the money when I start to receive the monthly payments?

Fortunately, the answer is no. This money will *never* become taxable to the contributor or to his/her heirs. The contributions are tax-deductible, the account grows with no taxes being taken out, and the retirement payments will be tax-free.

When the contributor dies, the payments will continue to his/her heirs on a tax-free basis with no estate or inheritance taxes.

13. Is it possible to contribute more than the 15.3% of earned income to the For America Security Trust (FAST) account?

The answer is YES!

First, for those that have earned income beyond the 15.3% of the tax cap (for 2020 it is $137,700), they can elect to contribute the 15.3% on all earned income with no upward limit and, remember, all contributions to the FAST are tax-deductible.

Second, everyone, whether they have earned income or not, can contribute up to $100,000 each year on a tax-deductible basis in addition to any 15.3% of payroll contributions.

These contribution limits have been structured this way with a two-fold purpose:

First, the 15.3% of earned income up to the payroll tax cap of $137,700 is there because it represents the amount that is currently taken from worker's paychecks. Working Americans will have the benefits of the FAST and it will not cost any more than they are currently paying for Social Security and Medicare taxes.

Second, the provision for the 15.3% of earnings over and above the $137,700 cap is there to encourage more money to come into the FAST as are the additional contributions of up to $100,000 annually. The more rapidly that the FAST grows, the more rapidly our nation's debts will be reduced and paid off.

NOTE: The $100,000 annual maximum is there because the purpose of the FAST is to benefit primarily low and middle-class Americans, not to provide a massive tax shelter for mega-wealthy billionaires.

14. Why are the benefits under the Plan For America (PFA) much greater than under Social Security?

This is an easy one. The benefits under the PFA are much greater because the participants enjoy the best parts of two worlds. The For America Security Trust (FAST) offers stock market returns for growth as well as government guarantees for safety.

15. How does the death benefit from Social Security compare with the Plan For America (PFA) plan death benefit?

Social Security: The actual cash death benefit from Social Security is very small, only $255. There is a provision for the surviving spouse and/or dependent children to receive monthly benefits until the children are no longer dependent and the spouse passes away. After the final benefits are paid out the Social Security Administration keeps all money that was paid in through the contributor's lifetime.

Plan For America: Under the PFA, the death benefit is the same as the living benefit. The heirs continue to receive the tax-free payments that will likely increase through the years for the rest of their lives and then pass it on to their heirs estate tax-free.

16. What protection will the Plan For America (PFA) retirees have from the ravages of inflation?

The PFA inflation protection features:

- The For America Security Trust (FAST) assets will be 100% invested in an index of the stock of U.S. corporations (large, medium, and small companies).
- According to Morningstar/Ibbotson, a highly regarded investment data service company, U.S. stocks (large company stocks) have about a 10.2% compounded annual rate of return over the last 94 years (1926 through 2019), and small company stocks have an even higher rate of return (11.9%).
- The rate of inflation for that period of time was 2.9%.
- Taking the 10.2% return and subtracting 2% for the annual FAST charge results in a net return of 8.2%.

- The 8.2% return easily surpasses the 2.9% historic rate of inflation.
- The FAST guarantees at least a 4% rate of return on retirees' investment accounts which also surpasses the 2.9% historic rate of inflation.
- Finally, the FAST also guarantees that the payout to retirees would be at a minimum at least equal to what they would be under Social Security, which is indexed to inflation.

17. What kind of report will the For America Security Trust (FAST) send out to the participants and how often?

Initially, the FAST will send out at least one report per year, which will indicate the current value of the individual's account and how the trust has performed in each year since the beginning. The report will also show the expected retirement benefits under each of the three methods of calculating those benefits.

First, the total of all of the participant's contributions to the FAST with a 4% compounded annual rate of return multiplied by 4% will be the guaranteed minimum annual retirement payout.

Second, the amount of Social Security that the participant would be eligible to receive would be the other guaranteed minimum payout.

Third, the accumulated value of the participant's account at the end of the previous year multiplied by 4% would be the retirement payout for the coming year.

The actual payout to the individual would be whichever of the three methods of calculation produces the highest number. It is anticipated in the future, as the FAST is fully established, that each individual's account value would be available electronically and, therefore, accessible on a more frequent basis.

The annual FAST report would also contain a proxy (a form for voting). The initial year of the FAST, the participants would have to vote for each of the five first-time trustees. Each year thereafter, the vote would be for one trustee to replace the one going off of the board unless circumstances caused there to be more than one trustee to leave the board in any year.

The number of votes that each participant would have would be the number of dollars in his/her account rounded to the nearest whole dollar.

18. Under Social Security, there are restrictions regarding how much an individual can earn, until a certain age is reached, without reducing the Social Security payout. Are there any restrictions under the Plan For America (PFA)?

The answer is simple. Unlike Social Security, there are no restrictions on any earnings whether it is earned income or investment income.

The benefits that flow from each individual's For America Security Trust (FAST) account belong to that individual and, under the contract that the FAST will have with the federal and state governments, those benefits cannot be restricted by arbitrary government rules or taxation.

It does not matter how much money a FAST retiree earns; it will not cause his FAST payout to be subject to taxation.

19. At what age can an individual start receiving his/her For America Security Trust (FAST) retirement payout?

Age 60 would be the earliest age (in a non-disability situation) where a FAST plan retiree could begin receiving monthly payouts.

- The decision would be up to the individual based upon how satisfied with the amount of payouts he/she would have at that age.
- There is a potential drawback to taking it at that early of an age if the individual plans on continuing to work. Like Social Security, once you elect to begin receiving benefits, you cannot switch back and forth between receiving benefits and deferring them.
- Under the FAST, once you elect to begin the payouts, then you will receive the payouts for the rest of your life.
- However, any earned income will still be subject to the 15.3% tax-deductible contribution up to the Social Security cap (presently $137,700). Optionally, the tax-deductible contributions can be extended to 15.3% of all earned income just like a pre-retirement individual. Also, up to an additional $100,000 can be contributed on a tax-deductible basis just as a pre-retirement individual.
- Importantly, every dollar contributed produces a four-cent permanent increase to the retirement payout on a guaranteed basis and is likely to be much more depending upon market performance.

Any retirement payouts that were received as the result of an inheritance commences at the time of the inheritance. The age of the beneficiary does not matter.

20. Why is it important that all of the companies listed in the For America Security Trust (FAST) index be required to be US domiciled (US based) corporations?

This requirement is in place because, as the name suggests, the FAST or For America Security Trust is to benefit the American people.

This requirement is important for two reasons:

> 1. It provides for uniformity, because all of the listed companies would have to comply with the same corporate law and accounting standards.
> 2. It benefits both the retirees as well as the working participants by recycling the tremendous capital flows back into the US stock markets.

> • All of this capital investment would help to provide employment opportunities for American workers.
> • Also, the steady investment flows would give support to the stock market, especially during times of economic weakness, in order to stabilize market returns and support retirement payouts.

21. Why is it important that the estate beneficiaries of the For America Security Trust (FAST) payouts be U.S. citizens, trusts set up for the exclusive benefit of U.S. citizens, bona fide U.S. based charitable organizations, government entities within the U.S. such as city, county, state or federal, or the FAST itself?

This requirement is important because the FAST is "For America" and the intent is to keep recycling the capital through the U.S. economy to not only benefit the current participants and retirees, but also future generations of U.S. citizens.

The exceptions to this rule would be:

- A spouse of a U.S. citizen that was not a U.S. citizen, he/she would continue to receive the retirement payout for the rest of his/her life.
- Dependent children of the deceased participant that were not U.S. citizens would continue to receive benefits until reaching adulthood.
- This does not mean that non-citizen spouses, children, or other heirs would be deprived of value from their inheritance. They would have the opportunity to sell the future payout cash-flow stream to a U.S. citizen for its fair market value.

Again, the intent is not to deprive any rightful heir of his/her inheritance but to keep the cash flows providing liquidity and growth to the U.S. economy, especially considering the fact that these cash flows are perpetual.

Chapter 9

Healthcare

1.What is the guiding principle for the universal healthcare under the Plan For America (PFA)?

The guiding principle for providing universal health care under the PFA is: "NO ONE, meaning the taxpayers, WOULD HAVE TO PAY FOR SOMEONE ELSE'S HEALTH CARE!"

2. What type of health insurance coverage would be available under the Plan For America (PFA)?

Comprehensive, high-quality healthcare insurance would be available to every U.S. citizen. The coverage under the "standard plan" would include, among other features, dental, orthodontic, vision, prescription drugs, hearing aids, long-term care (nursing home) and virtually any health care need. A $1,200 annual health savings account is included as an essential part of the "standard plan." Children can remain on their parents' plan up to age 26.

3.What is the "standard plan" and how would it work?

The "standard plan" is a high-quality, comprehensive health insurance policy that would include coverage for dental, orthodontic, vision, prescription drugs, hearing aids, extended care (nursing home), and virtually any healthcare need:

- It would include a health savings account in the amount of $100 per month or $1,200 annually.
- It would include a guaranteed insurability option for life and disability insurance.
- The maximum annual cost, aside from the premium, would be $1,200 for the combination of the co-pays plus the deductible — so that the health savings account would cover the total of the co-pays plus the deductible each year. Therefore, the annual premium would be the only out-of-pocket cost.
- Each insurance company that offered policies through the FAST would have to offer the "standard plan" but could do so with its own premium charge and with its own combination of co-pays plus deductible as long as it did not exceed the $1,200 each year.
- In addition to the "standard plan," the participating insurance companies could offer different variations in other policies.

The maximum insurance coverage under the "standard plan" would be $1,000,000; however, additional riders would be available to increase the coverage. This additional coverage would be available at normal rates without regard to pre-existing conditions or underwriting guidelines if purchased at the time of initial enrollment in the FAST. Otherwise, normal underwriting requirements would have to be met to avoid "adverse selection."

4.How are pre-existing health problems handled under Plan For America?

When the participant first enrolls in the For America Security Trust (FAST}, he/she would have the opportunity to purchase health insurance at the "standard plan" rate regardless of pre-existing health conditions, age, or occupation.

If an existing FAST plan policyholder wanted to switch to another insurance company, he/she would have to qualify in accord with the new insurance company's underwriting guidelines and give evidence of insurability in order to avoid what is called "adverse selection."

Adverse selection occurs when people with health problems want to buy insurance only after they find out that they have significant health problems, which is very negative for insurance company profitability.

5.What is the lifetime benefit under the "standard plan?"

The maximum lifetime insurance benefit under the "standard plan" is $1,000,000. Additional insurance riders would be available to increase the maximum ($2,000,000, $3,000,000 or more). If additional coverage was purchased at the initial enrollment, there would be no underwriting requirements. If, however, more coverage was purchased AFTER the initial enrollment, underwriting requirements would be mandatory to avoid "adverse selection."

6.What would happen if the maximum $1,000,000 payout was reached and the insured had not elected to increase his/her coverage?

The medical costs over $1,000,000 would be paid by the insured personally if he/she has the means to do so.

If the insured did not have the means to pay the medical costs, then the For America Security Trust (FAST) would grant the participant an interest-free loan to cover the medical cost with no ultimate cap on the amount.

If the participant was in the retirement/payout phase, his/her payouts would be reduced to the guaranteed amount and any amount over the guarantee would be used to repay the FAST.

- If the participant died before the loan was repaid, his/her spouse and/or dependent children would continue to receive the guaranteed minimum until the loan was repaid.
- If the spouse then died and the children were no longer dependent, the full amount of the monthly payment would go to the FAST until the loan was paid in full.
- If the loan amount exceeded the participant's balance in his/her FAST account, the guaranteed insurability purchase option for life insurance (that is part of the "standard plan") would be triggered and would increase the amount of life insurance each year so that the FAST balance plus the life insurance would= the total loan.
- The reasoning behind the loan balance being equal to the FAST balance Plus
- the life insurance is that, in a worst-case scenario, the FAST would recoup all of its money in 25 years (4% annual guarantee on 100% of the balance would pay off in 25 years).
- The life insurance premium rates for the guaranteed purchase options (for the purposes of guaranteeing the interest-free loans) are uniform regardless of age or sex; therefore, the life insurance would be affordable and would most likely be paid for via interest-free loans.
- Once the loan was fully repaid, the full amount of the monthly cash flows would go to the heirs.

If the participant was in the accumulation phase, then (as in the retirement phase) the life insurance purchase option would be triggered with no maximum as soon as the loan amount exceeded the balance in the participant's FAST account. Furthermore, the participant may also want life insurance for family protection and that could also be purchased. (The formula for life insurance purchase is in the section called Social Safety Net, question 7 in chapter 11). During the accumulation phase, any earnings on the participant's FAST account in excess of the guaranteed amount would be paid to the FAST as a loan repayment.

7. How are the health insurance premiums collected under the For America Security Trust (FAST) and how are they treated for tax purposes?

Under the FAST, plan the health insurance premiums, as well as life insurance and disability insurance premiums, would be paid by the policy owner via payroll reduction. Separate arrangements would be made for those who are not employed to either make payments or receive interest-free loans if they qualify.

All insurance premiums paid into the FAST would be 100% tax-deductible, both state and federal, with no means testing, no alternative minimum tax exposure, and no other present or future tax schemes to lessen this benefit.

8. What about policies other than the "standard plan?"

Competition and innovation should drive the insurers and the healthcare providers to market different plans that would serve varying markets. For example, some plans may broaden the definition of health care to cover alternative health care methods in addition to traditional medical care such as: acupuncture, chiropractic, holistic, nutrition, etc.

• The competition would stimulate innovation to drive costs down and efficiency up.

• Quality care would be ensured because multiple health care plans would be available as would many health care providers — all of them competing on quality and price.

• There would probably be a market for a higher cost premier type plan, but the tax deductibility would have to be limited to two times the "standard plan" so as not to be just a tax-avoidance gimmick.

9. How would the Health Savings Account (HSA) work?

The features of the Heath Savings Account would include:

• The health savings account would have a $100 per month premium that would be tax-deductible.

• Under the "standard plan," the $1,200 annual amount would be used to pay for the deductible and the co-pay requirements for healthcare services received during the course of the calendar year. The maximum amount of the deductible plus the co-pays would be $1,200 in any calendar year.

• If at the end of the year a portion of the $1,200 was not spent on healthcare, whatever is left over can be withdrawn tax-free.

• This will provide incentive to not overuse or abuse health care because each participant will be spending part or all of his/her own $1,200 tax-free dollars each year.

• Therefore, the amount spent on each healthcare service will probably be questioned. This should bring overall healthcare costs down but would, at the same time, provide assurance to the insured that affordability would not preclude him/her from getting whatever care was required.

10. What is the income qualification schedule to be eligible for the interest-free health care loans from the For America Security Trust (FAST)?

Each American citizen over the age of 26 (or under age 26 if not covered by a health insurance policy through a parent or guardian) would be eligible for an interest-free FAST loan to pay for his/her annual health insurance premiums in accord with the following schedule:

Annual Health Care Insurance Loan Schedule

Income - Lower Bound	Income - Upper Bound	Loan Amount (Percentage of Premium)
$0	$40,000	100%
$40,001	$50,000	75%
$50,001	$60,000	50%
$60,001	$70,000	25%
$70,001	—	0%

*It is important to note that the actual brackets will be more granular such that increasing wages never disadvantage the participant. For married couples filing jointly, these income boundaries are doubled.

11. What if a For America Security Trust (FAST) participant wanted to opt out of the health insurance part of Plan For America (PFA)?

The primary and most important point is the fact that participation in PFA is voluntary, not mandatory. However, if an individual participant wanted to opt out of the health insurance part of PFA, then he/she should have the right to do so.

It is important that the burden of the participant's health care expenses not be shifted to the taxpayer or anyone else via emergency room care.

To opt out, a participant would have to meet two requirements:

- First, the individual would have to place $100,000 in an investment or interest-bearing account under the control of the FAST to serve as a first line of defense against health care costs.
- Second, the opting out participant would be required to purchase a guaranteed insurability option to purchase the "standard plan" at the standard rate.

If the opting out participant had a health care expense that exceeded the $100,000 and could not cover it out of personal assets, then it would be paid with an interest-free loan from the FAST against his/her FAST account.

- The repayment of the loan would be in accord with the FAST policy for repayment of interest-free loans.
- Market returns in excess of the guarantees would go toward repayment of the loan.

If the opting out participant's investment account dropped below the $100,000 level for a 30- day period, the participant's option to purchase the "standard plan" would be automatically triggered.

12. What if an insurance company that was providing insurance through the For America Security Trust (FAST) got into financial difficulty?

If an insurance company that was providing insurance through the FAST got into financial difficulty, then that company could end up going bankrupt and its stockholders lose everything.

In the event of bankruptcy, the insurance policies would be taken over by competitors that offer insurance products through the FAST at their existing premium rates on a guaranteed basis with no penalty for pre-existing conditions.

The primary point is that no policyholder could lose his/her coverage and that the taxpayers would not have to pay for anyone else's healthcare.

13. Who should pay for the healthcare for non-U.S. citizen workers and their dependent families living in the USA?

Non-citizen workers and their dependent families, whether they be legal or not, need to be covered by health insurance because no one, meaning the taxpayers, should have to pay for anyone else's healthcare.

As it works now:

- From the standpoint of fairness, businesses and individuals have hired non-citizen workers primarily because they are willing to work for lower wages.
- When these workers and their families have healthcare needs, they use the emergency rooms of hospitals. The taxpayers, or other healthcare customers, wind up absorbing the cost through increased charges for paying patients.
- All U.S. citizens are subsidizing these individuals and businesses that get to hire this low-cost labor and have the rest of the people pay for it.

To remedy this situation:

- Employers should be held liable for the healthcare costs of their workers and dependent families if they are uninsured.
- If this requirement were in place, employers would then require proof of health insurance as a condition of hiring.
- The employers would be forced to pay higher wages because U.S. citizens would not be subsidizing their workers any longer.
- If the immigrants were paid higher wages, then it would be reasonable for employers to require health insurance as a condition for employment.
- This would apply to private individuals hiring a housekeeper as well as large corporations.

14. What if an individual U.S. citizen joined the For America Security Trust (FAST) at age 26, was never gainfully employed, had no assets and lived to age 86?

This individual would be covered by health insurance.

- He would have the guaranteed purchase option on disability insurance, but since he has no income to protect, it would not be activated.
- His guaranteed purchase option on the life insurance would be triggered because of the interest-free loan to pay the premium.
- The amount of the life insurance would increase as the loan balance for the health insurance increases.

Example:

- At his death (age 86) he would have 60 years of premiums at approximately $11,200 per year for a loan total of $672,000.

- The $672,000 of life insurance proceeds would be paid to the individual's FAST account.
- The guaranteed 4% payout from the FAST will ensure that the loan will be repaid in 25 years.
- Most likely, market returns will be greater than the guaranteed rate and the loan would be repaid much sooner than 25 years.
- After the loan is fully repaid, the annual cash flow would be paid to the individual's heirs.
- The FAST would only be missing out on the opportunity cost or time value of the money; but, with the 2% annual FAST charge (at a minimum would be $672,000 x 2%= $13,440 per year) in perpetuity, it would more than compensate the FAST for the loss on the time value of the money.

15. How will PFA help to contain rising healthcare costs?

PFA will help contain healthcare costs by:

- The tax-deductible $1,200 annual health savings account contribution, to be used for deductibles and copays, will be refundable tax-free to the extent that it is unused at the end of the year. This will help to reduce frivolous spending of healthcare dollars, but it will not limit spending for true healthcare needs.
- PFA will establish a one million lifetime insurance benefit cap for each American, unless additional insurance was purchased. If the $1 million cap is surpassed then all expenses would be paid from the income or assets of the insured until his/her assets have been depleted. Healthcare expenses thereafter would be paid by interest-free loans from the FAST. As these loans are issued there will be an equivalent amount of life insurance issued on a uni-sex, uni-age, guaranteed-issue

basis that will cover the ultimate repayment of the loan. This will strongly incentivize participants to closely watch how their health insurance dollars are being spent.

• Each healthcare provider serving insureds covered by PFA's insurance providers will be required to publish a menu of their services and the charges for each of those services. This will enable the insureds to become informed consumers of healthcare and to better husband the $1 million lifetime benefit from their insurance policy.

• All insurance policies from PFA providers will be available nationwide — both the policies and the benefits. The competition will help to keep prices in line with actual costs.

16. How will PFA handle healthcare inflation?

PFA will handle healthcare inflation by utilizing two different approaches:

1. The cost containment tactics outlined in the four steps in the previous question (healthcare #15) will have the effect of reducing some of the inflationary pressures or maybe actually bringing healthcare costs down.

2. The ultimate approach to the inflation problem would be to index the three key economic factors of the PFA healthcare provision. Index the lifetime $1,000,000 insurance cap.

• Index the premium payments along with the Health Savings Account (HSA) $11,200

• Index the income brackets which are the qualification for interest-free loans

Indexing is the ultimate protection for the PFA participant, but it is hoped that the four step cost containment measures will significantly reduce the need for a lot of indexing.

Chapter 10

Government Perspective

1. What is the greatest single benefit that the U.S. Government would derive from the implementation of the Plan For America (PFA)?

Although there are numerous benefits to the U.S. Government, the greatest single benefit from the implementation of the Plan For America would be the relief from an estimated $120 trillion in unfunded liabilities from the Social Security and Medicare programs.

Presently, the U.S. does not even have a plan on the "drawing board" for dealing with this problem. Even the so-called trust funds for Social Security and Medicare are nothing but U.S. Government notes which means they represent more government debt, not cash or investments.

$120 trillion is such a staggering sum of money that dealing with it, using the old method of just taking on more and more debt, is out of the question. The only economic engine powerful enough to carry such a load is corporate America. The For America Security Trust (FAST) will enable working-class Americans to enjoy widespread ownership in corporate America through the U.S. stock market.

In addition, the contract with the FAST provides for a U.S. Government guarantee so that the participants would have the best of both worlds: the stock market for growth and the U.S. Government for an ultimate guarantee.

The PFA contract with the Federal and State governments will relieve the governments of the obligations that they cannot meet and protect the American people from the past sins of the government.

2. Why is it essential that the For America Security Trust (FAST) be primarily established through a contractual agreement with the Federal Government and each of the 50 states rather than merely through legislation?

A contract is needed to protect us from the government. Any bill that is passed by the House of Representatives and the Senate and is then signed into law by the President can be changed or done away with by an opposite bill passed by the House of Representatives and the Senate and signed into law by the President. In other words, if we put in place a plan that solves America's retirement, health care, and debt funding problems but do not put in safeguards, then the government could do the same things that got us into this mess.

- It is absolutely essential that there be an inviolable iron-clad contractual agreement among the United States Government along with each of the fifty state governments and the For America Security Trust (FAST).
- The sacred trust of the people that the government has so egregiously violated must be safeguarded and taken permanently out of the government's hands.
- An independent board of trustees who answer only to the participants and beneficiaries of the FAST would

have the responsibility for the custody, administration, and investment of the FAST assets.

- There must be no government influence or ties to the board members or any of the key employees of the FAST.

- The strength and enforcement of this contract is the key to the permanency of the solution. If the Plan For America (PFA) strategy is implemented and the long-term obligations are handled, but the government is allowed back in, then "We the People" could find ourselves with an even more severe problem sometime in the future.

- If the government breaches the contract, then it should have to pay the $120 trillion (the amount of unfunded liabilities) to the FAST as the remedy.

An even more secure approach would be to make a constitutional amendment that keeps the people's retirement and health care funds separate from and off limits to the government.

3. What is the second greatest and immediate benefit to the Federal and State governments from the implementation of the Plan For America (PFA)?

The second greatest and immediate benefit to the Federal and State governments is being relieved of the Medicaid obligations. In 2019, the Federal Government spent about $406 billion on Medicaid and Obamacare. It is expected to grow 5.4% each year and reach $557 billion by 2025.

The individual states would be relieved of their portion of the Medicaid cost which in some states runs up to 17% of their annual expenditures see https://www.pewtrusts.org/en/research-and-analysis/articles/2020/01/09/states-collectively-spend-17-percent-of-their-revenue-on-medicaid). It might be possible for some states to balance their budgets with the removal of this large expenditure.

4. What is the best way to protect the Plan For America (PFA) benefits from the government?

A constitutional amendment is the best way because it would even further remove the PFA benefits from government access than a contractual agreement.

5. What would be the greatest ultimate benefit from the Plan For America (PFA) to the Federal and State governments?

The ultimate benefit to the Federal and State governments is the provision in the contract with the For America Security Trust (FAST) that calls for the cash flows from the FAST, once it has retired and paid off all of its bonds, to be paid to the Federal Government 50% and to the State governments 50%.

The annual cash flows from the FAST will retire its bonds between 2059–2079 depending on market returns. This amounts to trillions of dollars every year. These enormous cash flows will eliminate Federal and State debt and then ultimately replace taxation as the primary revenue source for government funding.

6. Why would the United States Government be willing to back the bonds issued for the For America Security Trust (FAST), pay the interest of the bonds, grant all of the various tax concessions in the contract, get out of the retirement and health care providing business as well as divesting itself of all equity stakes in any private enterprise that it holds?

The U.S. Government and the State governments should be ecstatic with this arrangement because they are getting a great deal.

- They will be relieved of almost $120 trillion in unfunded liabilities as well as the current Medicaid and Obamacare expenditures that are such a burden to the State governments.
- Additionally, a high-quality social safety net will be provided for all U.S. citizens without the enormous budget-busting outlays that are currently projected.
- The ultimate cash flows to government coffers to retire all debt and replace taxation as the primary revenue source should bring on outright jubilation from the Administration, Congress, and State politicians.

This deal would probably be regarded historically in the same league with the purchase of Manhattan Island for $24 in value, the Louisiana Purchase, or "Seward's Folly," the purchase of Alaska.

7. How would the Plan For America (PFA) eliminate the legal controversy regarding the "commerce clause" and the mandate to purchase health insurance?

The U.S. Supreme Court decided that Obamacare was a tax and therefore the law was constitutional. The Court did not rule on the constitutionality under the "commerce clause."

The PFA should not have any problem with this issue for the following two reasons:

First, the PFA is voluntary, therefore it does not rely upon a mandate to attract enrollees.

Second, the benefits offered under the PFA are so overwhelmingly superior to those offered by Social Security, Medicare, Medicaid, and Obamacare that the choice will be obvious.

The ultimate guarantee behind both the PFA and the existing Federal programs is the "full faith and credit" of the U.S. Government, but the PFA also has as a powerful funding source, the U.S. stock market, as its first line of defense; therefore, it is the safer approach.

8. How does the Plan For America (PFA) handle the issues of corporate governance and out-of-control executive compensation?

The PFA handles the corporate governance and out-of-control executive compensation through the proxy-voting process in contrast to the legislative approach.

Legislation is almost always done in response to a scandalous event that comes too late and is aimed at dealing with the previous problem, whereas the financial engineers, lawyers, and accountants on Wall Street are working on the next legal loophole to exploit.

In contrast, the proxy process established within the PFA would keep the corporations in the PFA portfolio under close scrutiny on a continuous basis and the penalties for improprieties would be swift and severe.

A proxy vote against the Board of Directors could terminate the board members and the top executives without waiting for a long and drawn out legal process. Transparency and accountability are the key elements in the PFA to make sure the corporate members of the PFA portfolio operate as good corporate citizens.

Let's look at the Proxy Vote and its Process:

The Proxy Vote and the Two Great Imperatives

The For America Security Trust (FAST) stock ownership brings the solemn responsibility to vote the proxies in a way that is most beneficial to the participants and beneficiaries.

The proxy is an authorization that is given to a representative to vote the shares (usually at a corporation's annual meeting). These corporate elections determine the make-up of the board of directors and other important policy decisions. The sanctity and transparency of this process is of critical importance to the long-term success and independence of the FAST.

The two great imperatives to protect the future of the FAST are: complete independence from any governmental control or influence and having safeguards in place that prevent corruption and self-dealing

The Process:

Once each year each participant/beneficiary of the FAST will be sent a proxy (ballot) to vote for one of the five trustees that would serve five-year terms and be term limited to one term only.

The number of votes that the participant/beneficiary would have would be determined by the number of dollars (rounded to the nearest dollar) in his/her FAST account.

The initial board would have terms that would run one year, two years, three years, four years, and one full five-year term. The initial board members with one, two, and three- year terms would be the exception to the one-term policy; they would be eligible to run for a full five-year term of their own after being off of the board for a period of three years.

The other exception would come about when a board member resigned or was removed before his/her term was completed. If the unfinished term was three years or less, then the incoming board member could serve a full five-year term after being off of the board for a period of at least three years.

These board members would have the responsibility for administering the entire FAST including the retirement, life, health, and disability insurance and any other functions or aspects of these programs.

- They are not government workers; they would be paid in line with private industry because "We the People" want the best talent available in order to get the best results.
- These trustees would be held to the highest standards and any breach of trust, malfeasance or ethical misconduct would be dealt with in the most severe criminal and civil prosecution.
- Since these board members serve at the pleasure of the participants, then an appropriate apparatus would be set up in order to have a special election to remove and replace any or all board members if the participants deem it to be necessary.
- The board members should have strong backgrounds, a wealth of experience, and a history of accomplishment as well as character that is impeccable.
- They must be free and independent from any government influence or control.

The board would appoint three-person mini-boards that would have the responsibility of analyzing, monitoring, reporting on, and voting the proxies of the companies in the FAST portfolio that they were assigned to.

- The exact number of companies these mini-boards could handle would be determined by the board itself.
- The specific companies that the mini-boards would have under their authority should change every 3 to 5 years in order to prevent corruption from developing as a consequence of a prolonged relationship between the corporation and the overseeing mini-board.

- The mini-board members should have expertise in finance, corporate governance, a good knowledge of the industries of the companies that they are overseeing, and a history of impeccable character.
- They should be well compensated in consideration of the tremendous responsibility that is placed upon them as well as the capabilities that they must possess.
- As is the case with the FAST board itself, these mini-board members would be held to the strictest standards and any misconduct or corruption would be dealt with harshly and prosecuted to the fullest extent of the law both criminally and civilly.

The FAST board will be responsible for hiring independent accounting and consulting firms to compile reports annually on the management and boards of directors of each company in the FAST portfolio.

- These comprehensive reports will evaluate the performance of the management and boards from the standpoint of long-term policies, financial condition, ethical behavior, compensation, and a host of additional criteria that these firms would devise to compare the quality of management that the investors are getting and the price (level of management and board compensation) that they are paying for it.
- Each comparison category- such as financial condition or long-term policies -would receive a letter grade as well as a composite letter grade for the company as a whole.
- The three-person mini-boards that vote the proxies on these companies for the FAST would be given these reports which they would use in addition to their own information to help them decide how to cast the proxy votes.

- They would then write up a report about how they intend to vote and why.
- The FAST board would then publish that report along with the report prepared by the accounting/consulting firm with the letter grades so that it would be public information and help other shareholders to make informed decisions when voting their shares.
- This process should go a long way in curbing excess management/board compensation and corporate abuse without government interference or mandate- because as the old expression goes, *"SUNLIGHT IS THE BEST DISINFECTANT."*

9. How could the Plan For America (PFA) resolve the dilemma of the unfunded retirement systems that plague many of the individual states?

The For America Security Trust (FAST) could resolve the underfunded retirement system's problems by taking over the state pension obligations. The takeover steps would be as follows:

The state would turn over its existing pension assets to the FAST and end its defined benefit pension plan.

The future pension contributions would be made by the state to the FAST on behalf of the retirement plan participant. The contribution amount would be a negotiated amount representing the change from an underfunded-defined benefit plan to a fully-funded defined contribution plan.

The state would be relieved of its pension obligations. This arrangement would be completely independent of the 15.3% payroll reduction that would be unaffected by this pension takeover.

The state workers would receive:

- A guaranteed benefit (backed by the "full faith and credit" of the U.S. Government) at retirement of 4% annually of the value of his/her account based upon a 4% compounded annual rate of return on all contributions made on his/her behalf.
- The 4% minimum return guarantee would extend permanently, and there would be a high probability that the returns would be significantly higher over time because the account would earn stock market returns less 2% (for the FAST charge) and the annual payout would be 4% of the previous year's ending account balance or the minimum guarantee whichever is greater.
- When the state employee retires, as early as age 60 at his/her option, then he/she would receive the monthly payout both federal and state tax-free.
- When the retiree passes away, his/her heirs would receive the tax-free cash flow that the retiree was receiving and it would pass to them without any estate or inheritance taxation instead of being forfeited as are most pension benefits currently.
- If the state was unable to convince its workers to accept the tradeoff of their partially-funded pension in exchange for the PFA, then the state could sweeten it by an additional amount added to the initial FAST contribution via a 2% interest rate deferred loan from the FAST to bring the participant's account up to the level that would make the deal acceptable. The loan would not require any annual payment by the state above the renegotiated pension contribution. The loan would accrue 2% interest compounded annually and would ultimately be paid off out of the state's share of the revenue sharing from the FAST after it had retired all of its bonds. No revenue sharing would be paid out to that state until the indebtedness and interest was paid in full. Of course, the

state would have the option of paying the loan off earlier if the state chose to do so.

10. What advantages and disadvantages would the states incur under the Plan For America (PFA)?

The advantages would be:

- Each state would be relieved of its Medicaid obligations to the extent that its citizens participate in the PFA (participation is likely to be nearly universal).
- Each state, if it elects, could be relieved of all of its pension liabilities both the funded and unfunded portions.
- Each state will receive its share of the *For America Security Trust* (FAST) revenues after all FAST bonds have been retired which will enable the state to ultimately retire all of its debt and reduce reliance on the taxation of its citizens.

The disadvantages would be:

- The loss of tax revenues (if the state has an income tax) on the FAST contributions representing 7.65% of the participant's earned income. If the participant's earned income is in excess of $137,700, then at his/her option 15.3% would be tax-deductible on contributions all the way up to the full amount of earned income, and those 15.3% of earnings would not be taxable by the state.
- The loss of tax revenue (if the state has an income tax) on the elective contributions, regardless of earnings, of up to $100,000 annually that a participant could contribute to the FAST on a tax-deductible basis.
- Each state's tax-free municipal bonds would have to compete with the tax-free dividends from the U.S. domiciled publicly-held corporations.

11. How will adopting the Plan For America (PFA) affect the goal of balancing the U.S. federal budget?

Adopting the PFA will affect the goal of balancing the US federal budget by removing the number one obstacle, which is spending on entitlements. If spending on Social Security, Medicare, Medicaid, and Obamacare are removed from the present and future budgets, then the excuses for deficit spending would be greatly diminished.

12. How will adopting the Plan For America (PFA) affect the goal of balancing the individual state budgets?

Adopting the PFA will affect the goal of balancing the individual state budgets in the near-term by removing Medicaid costs. In the longer-term, eliminating the unfunded pension liabilities along with Medicaid costs should take away the obstacles to balancing their budgets.

13. What happens to the enormous and building cash flows from the For America Security Trust (FAST) after all the federal and state debt is retired and the annual cash needs of the federal and state governments have been met?

The surplus cash flows generated from the FAST revenue-sharing would be refunded to all FAST accounts on a pro-rata basis from the federal surplus after all cash flow needs have been met.

The surplus cash flows from each state generated from the FAST revenue-sharing would be refunded to all FAST accounts in that state on a pro-rata basis from the state's surplus. This is important because, when that point in time comes, if the politicians are left with access to those gigantic cash flows, those politicians could once again become intoxicated with the ability to spend.

The people need to be aware that any excess spending is coming out of money that would otherwise be placed in their FAST accounts. This awareness and the tension between the people's interest and the politician's interest will hopefully keep spending in check.

Chapter 11

The Best Social Safety Net in the World

1. What will make the U.S. social safety net under Plan For America (PFA) the best in the world?

PFA makes the U.S. social safety net the best in the world because every U.S. citizen age 26 and over that elects to enroll in the plan will have a reasonably comprehensive financial plan provided for him/her. This is especially beneficial for those with very modest to moderate means.

2. What is meant by the phrase "a reasonably comprehensive financial plan?"

"A reasonably comprehensive financial plan" is a plan that deals with the five basic areas of financial planning, which are:

- Insurance planning-
    - Health insurance-
    - Long-term care insurance-
    - Disability insurance- Life insurance
- Investment planning
- Tax planning
- Retirement planning
- Estate planning

Many of the following questions in this Q&A section regarding the social safety net will specify how PFA meets these needs, but it is acknowledged that not every aspect of an individual's financial life is addressed through PFA, such as:

- Liability planning through property and casualty insurance
- Education planning for children
- Various other areas of people's financial lives.

3. Why is the main focus on the very-modest up through moderate-income American individuals and families?

The wealthy and upper-middle class can afford professional assistance in developing a financial plan for their futures. The lower-economic classes up through the middle class, however, are often the ones that need help the most yet cannot afford it. They are left on their own to financially plan their futures.

4. How does Plan For America (PFA) handle the health insurance aspect of the average American's financial plan?

PFA provides access to comprehensive health insurance for every U.S. citizen over 26 years of age that chooses to enroll in PFA, or under age 26 if he/she is no longer dependent upon a parent or guardian. This insurance coverage would be available on a guaranteed issue basis with no exclusion for pre-existing conditions.

Since this coverage would be purchased through the For America Security Trust (FAST), there would be no ultimate cap on the total benefits available for the health care that is needed.

The health insurance policy would be paid for through payroll reduction and would be 100% tax-deductible. A tax-deductible health savings account would be included as part of the policy. Any amount that was not used for health care cost (deductible plus co-pay) can be withdrawn tax-free at the end of the year as an incentive to not use the health insurance frivolously.

Some characteristics of PFA's health insurance plan are:

- The policy is individually owned.
- It is portable and usable in any part of the U.S.
- It is not tied to an employer.
- If the policyholder has very modest income or loses his/her job, he/she would be eligible for an interest-free loan so that the health insurance would remain intact regardless of economic circumstances.

Health insurance is one of the key parts of the financial planning puzzle that must be accessible on a continuous basis because, according to a 2001 Harvard study, about one-half of all personal bankruptcies are caused by healthcare costs.

5. How does Plan For America (PFA) handle the long-term care (nursing home care) aspect of the average American's financial plan?

PFA handles the long-term care needs as part of the health insurance coverage in the "standard plan." The health insurance premiums would reflect this coverage and the interest-free loan provision from the For America Security Trust (FAST) would take over if the policy maximum was reached and the participant did not have the personal means to deal with the long-term care expenses.

Consequently, PFA policyholders would not have to worry that their nursing home care in their elder years would be cut off because of lack of funding.

6. How does Plan For America (PFA) handle the disability income insurance aspect of the average American's financial plan?

PFA provides access to high-quality disability insurance to every plan participant in two ways:

First, at time of enrollment in PFA, a guaranteed-issue disability insurance policy would be available regardless of health status or occupation status.

Second, for those individuals not signing up for the disability insurance at time of enrollment, a guaranteed-insurability disability insurance purchase option would be required for all PFA participants.

The reason for this requirement, that every participant have either disability insurance or option to purchase disability insurance at the "standard policy" rate, is because disability insurance is required for any participant below retirement age to be eligible for an interest-free loan from the For America Security Trust (FAST) if it is ever needed.

This option would have a smaller premium than the premium for the disability insurance policy. The advantage would be the lower cost; but the disadvantage would be not having the coverage until the option was exercised and, even then, there would be a waiting period of maybe six months to avoid "adverse selection."

An individual could not wait until he/she became disabled and then exercise the option to get disability payments immediately. There would have to be a waiting period of maybe six months. Therefore, if it is affordable, it would be advisable to begin the insurance coverage at the time of enrollment.

The definition of disability would be the industry standard, not the Social Security definition. The "own occupation" standard would apply if it is applicable to the insured's occupation or profession.

The amount of disability insurance available through the FAST would be 60% of earned income as measured by the amount subject to the 15.3% contribution to the FAST (formerly known as the payroll tax amount).

- The maximum that would be covered by this policy would be 60% of the current payroll tax cap of $137,700.
- This amount would be reduced by the guaranteed payout from the insured's FAST account that would be triggered by the disability claim.

For example:

- If the insured's FAST account had a $200,000 balance at the end of the previous year, and the insured had $60,000 of earned income, the maximum payout would be 60% of $60,000 = $36,000 for the year or $3,000 per month. The $36,000 would come from the FAST payout and the disability insurance policy. With *$200,000 in the FAST account multiplied by 4% equals $8,000. The disability policy would provide $36,000 minus $8000 which equals $28,000*

- The payout would continue until recovery from the disability or until retirement age 65.

- At retirement age, assuming the disability was permanent, if the accumulation in the FAST account was not sufficient to produce an income at a 4% payout rate that would equal the disability income, then the disability payout would become the permanent retirement payout. The retirement payout would reach that level by means of an interest-free loan to the participant's FAST account.

For example:

To produce a $36,000 guaranteed payout at 4% would require $900,000 to be in the participant's account. The insured participant has $200,000; therefore, a $700,000 loan would be needed. This loan would be covered by $700,000 of life insurance that would be automatically purchased because of the interest-free loan.

The 60% payout maximum is necessary in order to avoid "moral hazard." This encourages the insured to return to the workforce when the disability is over.

All disability insurance benefit payouts purchased through the FAST would be tax-free.

If either the disability insurance or the guaranteed-purchase option is in force but the individual is not disabled, the insured's premium would rise or fall as his/her income increases or decreases. The potential for increase would stop when the 60%-of-salary-cap was reached. Also, if the FAST account reached the amount (as measured by the previous year's ending balance) that 4% of the amount equaled the face amount of the disability insurance, then the premium would decrease or even be eliminated.

The rate per $1,000 of the disability insurance would not increase or decrease, but the premium would rise, fall or be eliminated based on the amount of coverage in force.

If the FAST participant desires additional disability insurance beyond the limits offered through the FAST, then he/she could purchase it independently in the marketplace.

- Normal underwriting requirements would have to be met.
- The tax-favored status of PFA-purchased insurance would not be available to the insurance purchased outside of PFA.

7. How does Plan For America (PFA) handle the life insurance aspect of the average American's financial plan?

PFA provides access to life insurance on a guaranteed-issue "standard policy" premium basis regardless of health or occupation status at time of enrolling in PFA. The specifics are described below:

Similar to the disability insurance, there is a guaranteed insurability purchase option for life insurance that is required as part of the "standard policy" for those who elect not to purchase life insurance at the time of enrollment.

- The reason for this requirement — that every participant have either life insurance or the option to purchase life insurance at the "standard policy" rate — is because life insurance is required for any participant to be eligible for an interest-free loan from the For America Security Trust (FAST) if it is ever needed.
- The premium for the guaranteed life insurance purchase option would be lower than the premium for the

purchase of the life insurance itself, but exercising the option would include a waiting period to avoid "adverse selection" which occurs when an individual only purchases life insurance when he/she knows that there is a potentially life-threatening condition.

- The exception to the waiting period requirement would be triggered if an interest-free loan were granted to the participant by the FAST and the life insurance option had not been exercised prior to the loan being granted. This is to protect the FAST against unpaid loans.

The life insurance policy would be similar to a reducing term policy calculated to provide 60% of earned income up to the current tax cap of $137,700.

- This amount would be reduced by the amount that would've been added to the participant's FAST account value at the end of the previous year.
- This amount would increase as the participant's annual earned income increases up to the maximum of 60% of the $137,700 cap, minus the value of the participant's FAST account value at the end of the previous year.
- Once 4% of the FAST account balance equaled or exceeded the 60% of earned income level, the premium would stop and there would be no coverage or premium unless the 4% of the FAST balance fell below the 60% of earned income level.
- The life insurance premium per $1,000 of coverage would be uniform regardless of health, gender, age or occupation.

For example:

- If the current value of the participant's FAST account was $200,000 and the annual earned income was $60,000.
  - 60% of $60,000 = $36,000
  - $200,000 FAST balance multiplied by 4% = $8,000
  - $36,000 — $8,000 = $28,000
  - To provide $28,000 of annual income (with a guaranteed 4% payout rate) to the heirs of the participant would require $700,000 of life insurance proceeds.
  - The $700,000 from the life insurance plus the $200,000 FAST balance= $900,000
  - $900,000 multiplied by 4% = $36,000 annual tax-free guaranteed benefit to the heirs.

The reason for the 60% of earned income cap is to not create a "moral hazard" where the family would have a greater economic benefit from the tax-free cash flow from the FAST than the insured was earning on an after-tax basis.

If a PFA participant desires additional life insurance, then he/she could purchase it in the marketplace, not through the FAST. However, normal underwriting requirements would have to be met and the tax-favored status of PFA-purchased life insurance would not be available.

The life insurance purchased to cover an interest-free loan from the FAST would not be impacted or limited by the earned income calculations as in the above example.

8. How does Plan For America (PFA) handle the retirement planning aspect of the average American's financial plan?

PFA handles the retirement aspect of the average American's financial plan through the same 15.3% of earned income that is presently collected as the payroll tax.

- For those individuals that enroll in PFA, the 15.3% of their earnings would be withheld and deposited into the For America Security Trust (FAST) and then credited to his/her individual FAST account.
- The money contributed to this account would be invested in a portfolio of all U.S. domiciled stocks similar to a total-market stock index.
- The participant's return would be the market rate of return less 2% paid to the FAST as a charge for the plan administration and the 4% guaranteed return.
- The cash flow at retirement would be determined each year as the greatest of the three options:

1. The present level of Social Security benefits.
2. 4% of the total of all of the participant's contributions to the FAST made over his/her lifetime plus a 4% compounded annual rate of return.
3. 4% of the total accumulation in the participant's FAST account at the end of the previous year.

9. How does Plan For America (PFA) aid in the investment planning aspect of the average American's financial plan?

PFA participant would be automatically saving and investing at least 15.3% of his/her earned income into the For America Security Trust (FAST) and deducting it from his/her taxable income.

Also, if the participant has earned income exceeding the $137,700 tax cap, then he/she could elect to have 15.3% of earnings over the tax cap up to the total amount earned contributed to his/her FAST account.

In addition, to the extent that it was affordable, he/she could invest up to $100,000 annually into his/her FAST account and have it be tax-deductible.

If the FAST participant wanted to invest some money but was not in a position to put any extra money into the retirement account, then investing in U.S. publicly-traded stocks, stock mutual funds, or exchange traded funds that held U.S. publicly-traded stocks would produce dividends that would be tax-free, thereby enhancing the returns.

10. How does Plan For America (PFA) aid in the tax planning aspect of the average American's financial plan?

PFA incorporates many tax benefits into its basic structure to benefit all Americans.

- All insurance premiums paid through the For America Security Trust (FAST) through payroll reduction would be tax-deductible whether these premiums were for health, disability, or life insurance.
- All payments for the health savings account would be tax-deductible, and whatever amount was left unspent on medical care (deductibles plus co-pays) at the end of the year could be withdrawn tax-free.
- The 15.3% of earnings contribution up to the $137,700 cap would be tax-deductible.
- The 15.3% of earnings contribution over the $137,700 cap is optional but, if opted for, would be tax-deductible.
- The optional contribution of up to $100,000 over and above the 15.3% of earnings would be tax-

deductible. The $100,000 limit is in place to primarily benefit lower up through middle-class taxpayers and not mega-wealthy billionaires.

- All insurance proceeds from policies purchased through the FAST would be tax-free (health, disability, or life).
- All retirement payouts from the FAST account would be income tax-free to the participant and income and estate tax-free to the heirs.
- Dividends of U.S. domiciled publicly-traded corporations would be tax-deductible to the corporation and tax-free to the recipient, both federal and state.

11. How would Plan For America (PFA) provide a legacy for each participant that contributed?

Each U.S. citizen that has contributed to the For America Security Trust (FAST) would have a legacy to leave to his/her heirs.

The surviving spouse and dependent children would receive the full amount of income from the deceased's FAST account for the balance of his/her lifetime.

After that the monthly cash flow would be paid out to the beneficiaries of the original participant. It would be the greater of:

- 4% of the total contributions to the FAST plus a 4% compounded rate of return.
- 4% of the balance at the end of the previous year.
- The third option, the present level of Social Security benefits, is not available to the heirs. It is only available to the original participant and spouse or dependent children.

- The heirs would be delayed in receiving any benefits until all outstanding interest-free loans from the FAST had been fully repaid.
- Once the loans had been repaid, the heirs would receive the full amount of the cash flows — income and estate tax-free — which is the legacy of the original participant.

12. What characteristic would distinguish Plan For America (PFA) from most of the nations of the world's social safety nets?

PFA is based on individually owned and individually-funded insurance policies and retirement accounts. The funding is accomplished through payroll contributions and/or interest-free loans that are ultimately paid back from the cash flow from the individual's For America Security Trust (FAST) account.

The FAST account is individually owned and funded, whereas most nations have government owned, controlled and funded plans. This unique characteristic enables PFA's participants to pass the wealth that they have accumulated on to their heirs in the form of tax-free cash flow because the account is not with the government and is not ceded to the government upon death.

The 'Plan For America'

How to Place the American Dream on a Sure
Foundation Forever

Part III

Proof

Chapter 12

The Numbers

Now that you know how Plan For America works, you might be saying to yourself, "That all sounds great in theory, but what is the proof?" The numbers in this part of the book are generated by an econometric model built in conformity with Congressional Budget Office and Social Security Administration assumptions. One of the assumptions is a 6.2% average annual market return, which is significantly below the actual historic average of 10.2%. Plan For America still works under this lower return scenario, and this report shows numbers for both 6.2% and 10.2% assumptions.

The following is a reprint of the original white paper.

Evaluating the Feasibility of Plan For America

Kyre Dane Lahtinen, Ph.D.2

Funding for this study was provided by Plan For America.

The author maintained complete control over the methods, analysis, and conclusions of this paper. Any consultation between the author and Plan For America served only to clarify points of fact related to the design of the plan, plan terminology, and other objective points. 2The author is an Assistant Professor of Finance. This work was completed external to his regular university employment.

June 22, 2020

This paper examines the key features and feasibility of the Plan For America.

Background

The current fiscal situation of the United States federal government raises red flags for a wide variety of reasons. For example, even before the outbreak of SARS-CoV-2, the Congressional Budget Office (CBO) projected the federal deficit for 2020 to be larger than $1 trillion. The pandemic will add trillions of dollars to already ballooning deficits. CBO estimates from before the pandemic projected the annual deficit to increase to $1.7 trillion by the year 2030 and reach a staggering $7.7 trillion by the year 2050.

The effect that these consistently increasing budget deficits have on the national debt is alarming. Before the pandemic, the CBO projected federal debt held by the public for 2020 to be $17.9 trillion. This is expected to increase to $31.4 trillion by the year 2030 and reach a staggering $116.6 trillion by the year 2050. For better scale, the CBO projected debt in 2020 to be 81% of GDP but grow to 180% of GDP by 2050. The pandemic will only make each of these projections worse, once the CBO accounts for its effects.

Plan For America is an effort to fix the long- term financial issues of the United States of America listed above. Specifically, Plan For America (PFA) is designed to replace Social Security, Medicare, and Medicaid with a sustainable long-term solution that is built on top of sound investment management and free mar- ket principles. By instituting replacement pro- grams, PFA aims to provide for retirement, dis-ability, and health benefits for all Americans, retire the national debt, and become a sustain- able funding source for federal and state governments.

This report is an examination of PFA and a look into its key provisions to determine the plan's feasibility and the potential PFA has to overcome the current unsustainable trajectory of the federal budget and the federal debt. The rest of the paper is organized as follows. Section 2 describes the key features of PFA. Section 3 evaluates the cash flow potential of PFA. Section 4 lays out the strengths of the plan. Section 5 discusses key questions about the plan going forward. Section 6 concludes the paper.

Key Aspects of PFA

To understand how PFA plans to replace Social Security, Medicare, and Medicaid, I will discuss the main features of the plan, including, its le- gal structure, the funding source, the Social Security replacement, the Medicare and Medicaid replacement, revenue generated by PFA, and the application of any PFA revenue.

PFA will be created as its own private entity, which has obligations to the federal government, state governments, and its plan participants through the use of a legal contract, rather than through legislation. PFA prefers this structure so its funds will sit outside of the reach of the political structure, and, therefore, will be used only for their intended purposes.

PFA is funded by using existing Federal Insurance Contributions Act (FICA) payroll taxes as contributions to individual accounts. For these taxes, employers and employees each currently contribute 6.2% for Social Security and 1.45% for Medicare, totaling 15.3% of wages. As this 15.3% of earnings will be going to fund PFA ac- counts they will no longer be considered taxes, and they will be tax-deductible to individuals.

PFA replaces Social Security by creating an individual account for each worker held in a trust called For America Security Trust (FAST). These individual FAST accounts are funded each year by the FICA payroll tax equivalents mentioned above. The funds are placed in a market-participating account that holds a broad-based index fund, such as one that might track the Wilshire 5000. This ensures investors are properly diversified and reduces costs of managing the plan. When workers reach retirement age, they receive distributions from their account. Distributions are capped to a maximum percentage of the FAST account value and retirees cannot withdraw additional funds above these limits. For most retirees, the distribution will be 4% of their FAST account per year, however, the full PFA plan describes scenarios where the distribution can be as high as 5%. When retirees die, they pass their benefit on to chosen beneficiaries. The benefit is passed on indefinitely from one beneficiary to the next.

Crucially, PFA makes several guarantees to plan participants. First, PFA guarantees that plan participants will receive a retirement benefit equal to or greater than what they would have received under Social Security. Second, PFA guarantees that participants will earn no less than an average of 4% compounded on their FAST account per annum over the duration of the account.

PFA replaces Medicare and Medicaid using private health insurance. These insurance policies have a flat premium across the board. Individuals who are unable to afford their health insurance premium are given interest-free loans to cover their premiums. These healthcare loans are either paid off as the FAST account of the individual generates excess returns during the life of the individual or they are paid off using the residual retirement benefit after the person dies. In some circumstances, an individual's FAST account will not be large enough to cover their health care loans, so a life insurance policy that is paired with the health insurance policy covers their remaining health care debt.

Table 1: *Key Model Inputs*

Variable	Assumption
Age Enters Workforce	20
Retirement Age	65

Life Expectancy	78
Income Dist.	2021
FICA Taxes	15.3%
Market Return	6.2%
Health Insurance Premium	$11,200
FAST Fee	2%
Wage Growth	3.5%

PFA generates revenue each year to help cover its operating and other expenses. This revenue comes from a fee that is charged as a percentage of assets under management. The fee is charged on the current balance of all FAST accounts. The revenue PFA generates from its management fee can be used to cover the cost of the various guarantees of the plan. A more detailed discussion of the fee's uses follows later in this section.

For a more detailed look at the PFA's policies an interested reader should consult http://planforamerica.us/qa/. There you will find more specific details about PFA's design. For example, the distribution structure is laid out in more detail and the rules regarding when a plan participant may take a 4% versus a 5% distribution are described. Full de- tails regarding what basic coverage the health insurance guarantees, including discussion on pre-existing conditions and lifetime limits. Additionally, the full plan also discusses important topics such as how PFA will manage voting the shares that are held in the trust and other corporate governance issues.

Table 2: *Health Care Loan Schedule*

Lower Bound	Upper Bound	Loan Amount
$0	$40,000	100%
$40,001	$50,000	75%
$50,001	$60,000	50%
$60,001	$70,000	25%
$70,001	–	0%

Plan Evaluation

To evaluate the feasibility of PFA I establish a base scenario. This base scenario depends on conservative estimates for all key inputs to the model. For example, the assumed nominal market return of 6.2% is far below the historical average, and, therefore, stretches out the time it takes for the plan to break even. The market return of 6.2% is the rate sources say is typically required by the Congressional Bud- get Office to evaluate the growth of the market in future projections. Market returns higher than the assumed rate and closer to the historical average would improve the outlook for PFA. The key inputs are found in table 1. To illustrate how these key inputs determine the success of PFA, I will follow the lifecycle of a hypothetical plan participant. All aggregate projections assume the plan is enacted and fully implemented, meaning 100% voluntary participation.

The plan participants are assumed to enter the workforce at age 20. The participant is as- signed a beginning wage based on the income distribution from 2021. At the end of each calendar year of the working life of the participant, several calculations are made that affect the participant's FAST account.

First, PFA calculates the annual management fee of 2% based on the ending balance of the FAST account. Next, the participant's annual contribution is determined. This is equal to their wages multiplied by the FICA tax rate of 15.3%.

Next, I determine if the participant qualifies for health care loans to cover the cost of their health insurance premium, which is assumed to be $11,200 per year, which includes the $1,200 health savings account contribution. Health care loans are granted based off of the information found in table 2. For example, if someone earns less than $40,000 per year, then they can borrow 100% of the money to pay their premium. Whereas, if someone earns $55,000 they can only borrow 50% of the money for their premium. In the actual plan implementation, the brackets will be more granular such that in- creasing wages never disadvantage the individual. If the individual qualifies for a health care loan, the amount is added to the participant's overall loan balance. This finalizes the end of year calculations and adjustments. The participant's wages then grow by the annual wage growth rate of 3.5%. The end FAST account balance then grows at the assumed market rate of return of 6.2%. This cycle repeats until the person reaches the retirement age of 65.

Once in retirement, the individual begins taking distributions from their FAST account equal to 4% of their account balance. The individual may continue to receive health care loans according to table 2, except now count- ing their FAST account distributions against the loan schedule instead of their earned income.

This continues until the participant dies, at which time one of two things occur. If the participant has a remaining health care loan balance then the distributions begin to pay off the balance of the health care loans. After such time that the health care loans are paid off, or if the participant dies with no remaining health care loan balance, then the 4% distribution is passed on to surviving predesignated beneficiaries.

The model follows the expected population of the United States through this hypothetical cycle until the year 2100 and aggregates the results for a comprehensive look at the potential total impact of PFA. Note that any comparisons that are made between PFA's performance and those of expected outlays by the Federal Government are sourced from the Congressional Budget Office Long Term Budget Outlook that was updated in February of 2020.

Figure 1: *FAST Balance*

(in billions)

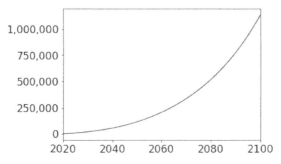

This long-term update is somewhat less precise than previous projections. Future expected values are grouped into multi-year blocks; these multi- year blocks cause many of the charts in this analysis to take a jagged shape. This update also only forecasts the budget until 2050, whereas previous updates had longer term forecasts. To compensate for this, I project forward the relevant figures until the year 2100 using the latest set of CBO projections. The jagged nature of the most recent CBO estimates also cause what may seem like unusual trends in the tables in the appendix of this white paper. To reiterate, the unusual rise or fall in numbers that depend on the CBO should be expected.

As noted above in table 1, I employ a static value for wage growth throughout the projection. I made this choice as a trade-off between complexity of the model or its exact tracking of CBO projections. So, I chose the simpler model with fewer assumptions. This leads to estimates of contributions to the FAST accounts that are slightly biased downward for the duration of the model. The net affect is that the plan is biased downward over its modeled period.

Figure 1 shows the overall growth of the ag- gregate FAST accounts. The slope of the curve is non-linear, it curves upward, and reflects the impact of compounding interest on the FAST ac- counts. The aggregate FAST accounts become quite large, passing $100 trillion by 2046. This occurs because of the large contributions, the

Figure 2: *Expected Annual Social Security Payout Minus FAST Account Payouts*

(in billions)

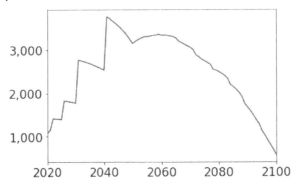

contributions in the first year of the plan are over $1 trillion, and because no principle can be withdrawn from the FAST accounts.

As mentioned above, PFA guarantees that the distributions made to retirees will meet or exceed what they would have received under the Social Security system. As the distributions represent 4% of the account value of the retiree, the distributions for people currently in retirement or close to retirement age when the plan begins will need their distributions supplemented in order to be the same as Social Security. Figure 2 shows the annual deficits be- tween expected Social Security payouts and the distributions from the FAST accounts. The regular 4% distributions exceed the amount that would have been paid under Social Security just outside the time range included in this model. Note that the cross-over point for the FAST distributions relative to Social Security is so far out into the future due to a mismatch be- tween the assumptions that the Congressional Budget Office (CBO) makes about the growth rate of Social Security benefits and the assumptions about the 6.2% market rate of return in the model. For example, the CBO assumes an average annual growth rate of Social Security benefits of approximately 4.5%. This growth is due to inflation increasing the payouts and a larger percentage of the population drawing benefits. This makes the assumption of a

Figure 3: *Health Care Loan Balance*
(in billions)

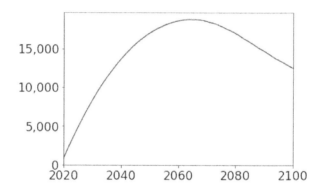

market return of 6.2%, which sources indicate is required by CBO for evaluating market projections, extremely conservative, as the spread between inflation and the market rate of re- turn is usually much larger than the difference between the growth rate of Social Security benefits and 6.2%. Using a market rate of return of 10.2%, which is closer to the historical average for equities, would more appropriately match the CBO's projections about growth in Social Security benefits. Using the higher market rate of return moves all break-even points significantly closer to the present time.

Figure 3 shows the growth in aggregate health care loans through time. The health care loans grow rapidly in the early years of PFA. The loan growth rate is increasing for the early life of PFA but begins to decline as individuals begin to pay off their loans. PFA allows for excess FAST account growth to be used to payoff health care loans during the life of the individual, where excess returns would be any account growth above the 4% rate of return the plan guarantees. Therefore, as we are using a market rate of return of 6.2% and a fee amount of 2%, there would be 0.2% available each year to pay down an individual's health care loans. However, this base model examination of PFA restricts the payoff of loan balances until after the individual becomes deceased. Therefore, the 0.2% continues to grow within the account. This simplifying assumption has two effects:

Figure 4: *Annual FAST Fee*
(in billions)

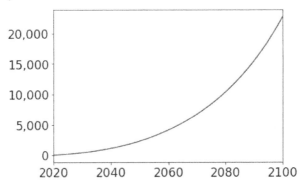

Figure 5: *Aggregate FAST Fee*

(in billions)

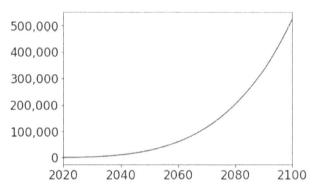

one, it causes the health care loan balances to grow more rapidly than they would other- wise grow, because there are no payments being made, and two, the FAST accounts grow more rapidly, because funds are not being used to pay down the health care loans during an individual's life. These two forces counteract each other and should not change the interpretation of the performance of PFA.

Figure 4 details the growth of the annual FAST account management fee. This fee is 2% of assets under management. PFA specifies that the funds generated by this fee are primarily to be used for several things. First, the fees can be used to help offset any shortfall the plan may experience from the guarantee that all retirees will receive at least what they would have received under Social Security.

Second, the fees can be used to offset any shortage in market rates of return that would prevent the participants from earning at least 4% on their FAST account. Third, the fees can be used

Figure 6: *Social Security Break-even*
(in billions)

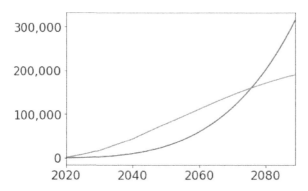

as a source of funding for health care loans and to retire any bonds PFA issued previously to provide health care loans. And, fourth, the fees could be provided to federal and state governments as a supplementary funding source for their budgets to first pay off debt and then supplement regular spending. Figure 5 shows the aggregate FAST account fees charged up to any point in time. This is to illustrate the aggregate amount of additional resources the fees generate.

Ultimately, the potential success of PFA de- pends on answering several key questions. Can the fee cover the shortfall the plan incurs due to guaranteeing a payout equal to Social Security or greater? Can the plan produce the cash flows required to make the needed healthcare loans? If the plan is able to cover its associated costs, how long does it take to reach these break-even points?

Figure 6 shows the relationship between the aggregate Social Security deficit and the aggregate FAST fee. The Social Security deficit comes from the difference between what the FAST accounts distribute and the projected pay- outs for Social Security benefits. As shown in figure 2, FAST accounts begin to

138

distribute more than Social Security just outside the time range included in this model; the aggregate Social

Figure 7: *Health Care Loan Break-even* (in billions)

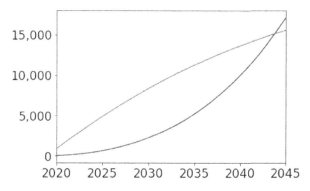

Security deficit reaches its maximum value of approximately $100.0 trillion the year prior. Figure 6 shows that, if the FAST fees are used exclusively to pay off the Social Security deficit, the deficit will be paid off by the year 2075.

Figure 7 shows the relationship between the aggregate health care loan balance and the aggregate FAST fee. Recall that the loans are made to individual citizens who are ultimately responsible for paying them back; PFA is not responsible for paying them back. However, PFA still requires a financing source to be able to make the loans. Therefore, PFA must borrow in order to lend to the individuals. If PFA used the cash flows generated by the FAST fee as the source of funds to make new health care loans, then there would be enough capital avail- able by the year 2044 to wholly self-finance the health care debt, again assuming that the fees were used exclusively to finance the health care loans.

Figure 8 shows the total cash flow needs of PFA when the Social Security deficit and the health care loans are considered together. Using the FAST fee to cover both of these uses of funds results in reaching break-even in the year 2079. Note that the break-even point in time for covering both uses of funds is not significantly longer than covering the costs of either uses of funds individually; this is the case because the FAST fee grows extremely rapidly and becomes quite large, as shown in figures 4 and 5.

Figure 8: *Combination Break-even*
(in billions)

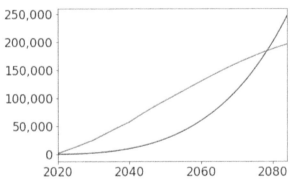

The main conclusion from the analysis of these three break-even points is that PFA is self-sustaining from its inception and has com- pletely paid back its borrowing by the year 2079.

The projected PFA cash flows under the base case scenario considered can be found in ta- ble 3 at the end of this paper. Reading across the table you can follow the life cycle of the aggregate FAST accounts just as is described in this section. Participants contribute funds to the FAST accounts, they take payouts if they are in retirement, they borrow money to cover their health care premiums, their accounts make pay- outs to cover their health care loans after they die, their accounts distribute funds to their beneficiaries in the form of a residual payout, the FAST account balance grows, the total health care borrowing increases, and the annual FAST fee is charged.

The total projected borrowing that the PFA would require can be found in table 4. This table follows the amount of shortfall generated by the Social Security Guarantee and the amounts necessary to finance the health care loans, while comparing it to the aggregate fees charged on FAST accounts.

For the information of the reader, tables 6- 8 repeat the analysis mentioned in this paper but use a market rate of return of 10.2%. This higher rate of return is closer to the historical average for the market and more inline with the

Figure 9: *Social Programs Deficit*
(in billions)

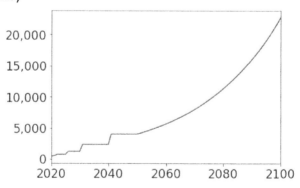

economic assumptions made by the Congressional Budget Office for the future expected expenses of Social Security, as previously noted. Obviously, using a higher market rate of return makes PFA significantly more attractive as it moves all break-even points up several years and increases the fees collected by the trust. For example, the Social Security break-even moves up to 2058, the health care loan break- even moves up to 2039, and the combination break-even point becomes 2059.

Plan Strengths

The evaluation of PFA showed that it can be a viable alternative plan to provide for the retirement and health care needs of the American people. Beyond the simple observation that the plan's cash flows appear to be sustainable, there are several strengths that I perceive in the plan and in its implementation.

First, PFA uses existing funding sources. Instituting PFA means no change to an individual's or a business's tax burden. PFA repurposes existing funds in a more efficient manner.

Second, PFA links revenues and liabilities. Each individual in the plan provides cash flows for their own retirement. The health care loans an individual takes out are paid off by cash flows from their own FAST accounts. This gets rid of unfunded liabilities. Regardless of the balance of the health care loans, there is the certainty of specific cash flows to pay them off. Regardless of fluctuation in the population of the United States or the composition of the work- force, individuals will be providing for their own retirement.

Third, PFA covers the health care and retirement needs for all people. This is the end goal that most people want to see. PFA achieves it without some of the distortions that many people fear about such systems.

Fourth, PFA would remove the largest future contributors to the national debt, namely Social Security and

Medicare/Medicaid, from the federal budget, thus alleviating our budget cri- sis. Additionally, PFA would generate revenue available to cover national and state debt and pay it off. Figure 9 shows how much Social Security, Medicare, and Medicaid contribute to the federal deficit over the next 70 years. PFA would completely remove this from the budget narrowing the federal deficit significantly.

Table 5 illustrates the direct effects PFA would have on the Federal budget. The Federal budget would begin to experience a surplus in the first year PFA is fully implemented. This is the case because the combined social programs are a main cause of the current deficit. Under cur- rent projections, the Federal budget would see a surplus beginning in the year 2021 if PFA were enacted and fully implemented, and, after running surpluses for some time, deficits would return in 2048, due to projected increases in discretionary spending. However, as the excess FAST Fee gets distributed to the Federal Government, surpluses return in the year 2079. Additionally, non-social spending outpaces the revenue the government collects. Although PFA borrowing does grow to a significant amount, it is dwarfed by the amount of Federal debt that the country is expected to carry. PFA would significantly reduce the trajectory of the Federal debt by turning the Federal deficit into a surplus. PFA's Remaining Questions

PFA's success in the base case scenario explored in this paper is an indication that the PFA is worth exploring further. Even though I have approached the question about how likely the plan is to succeed given a certain set of assumptions, many other questions remain before the plan could be implemented.

One potentially major question would be the impact that such large and ongoing cash inflows would have on financial markets. Early in PFA's life the annual contribution would be approximately $1 trillion dollars contributed to the FAST accounts each year. This money is then invested in broad based index funds. However, as noted above, the principal cannot be with- drawn, and, therefore, the money locked inside FAST accounts will grow until they become the vast majority of the value of the overall market. This is problematic because how efficient can markets be when an increasingly large percent- age of funds are locked into the market and have no ability to leave or even switch between asset classes? This needs to be explored more fully before PFA can be implemented.

Obviously, the political workability of PFA is still an outstanding question. Although, the plan does satisfy many requirements of people with diverse political views and backgrounds. However, this may be less of a concern as the current pandemic alters voters desire for strong action both in the healthcare and in fiscal responsibility.

Conclusion

In this paper I examine the Plan For America, a plan to replace Social Security and Medi- care/Medicaid programs of the United States with a viable long-term solution. Using a conservative base case scenario, I show that PFA's fundamental ideas do produce a self-contained replacement program that can provide for the retirement and healthcare needs for the country. Instituting PFA would not only open the door to fixing federal and state budget deficits, but also eventually retiring the national and state debt.

Plan For America

This table contains the projected PFA cash flows under the base case scenario considered in this paper. Reading across the table you can follow the life cycle of the aggregate FAST accounts just as is described in section 2. "Year" indicates the year to which the data correspond. "Beginning FAST Balance" is the aggregate balance of all FAST accounts at the beginning of the year. "Contribution" is the amount FAST participants contribute to their accounts, which is 15.3% of their wages. "FAST Retirement Payout" represents the amount that gets distributed to retirees from their FAST accounts. "FAST Residual Payout" is the amount that gets paid out to the designated beneficiaries after the original account holder has passed. "Healthcare Loan Repayment" is the amount paid toward outstanding healthcare loans by plan participants. "FAST Balance Plus 6.2% Growth" is the account value after combining the beginning balance with the contribution and allowing it to grow at 6.2%. "FAST Fee" is the annual 2% management fee. "Ending FAST Balance" is the market value of the FAST accounts at the end of the year. See page 4 for a discussion on the jagged nature of these projections. All values are reported in billions of dollars.

Table 3: *PFA Cash Flows Assuming 6.2% Market Return*

This table contains the projected PFA cash flows under the base case scenario considered in this paper. Reading across the table you can follow the life cycle of the aggregate FAST accounts just as is described in section 2. "Year" indicates the year to which the data correspond. "Beginning FAST Balance" is the aggregate balance of all FAST accounts at the beginning of the year. "Contribution" is the amount FAST participants contribute to their accounts, which is 15.3% of their wages. "FAST Retirement Payout" represents the amount that gets distributed to retirees from their FAST accounts. "FAST Residual Payout" is the amount that gets paid out to the designated beneficiaries after the original account holder has passed. "Healthcare Loan Repayment" is the amount paid toward outstanding healthcare loans by plan participants. "FAST Balance Plus 6.2% Growth" is the account value after combining the beginning balance with the contribution and allowing it to grow at 6.2%. "FAST Fee" is the annual 2% management fee. "Ending FAST Balance" is the market value of the FAST accounts at the end of the year. See page 4 for a discussion on the jagged nature of these projections. All values are reported in billions of dollars.

Year	Beginning FAST Balance	Contribution	FAST Re-tirement Payout	FAST Residual Payout	Healthcare Loan Repayment	FAST Balance Plus 6.2% Growth	FAST Fee	Ending FAST Balance
2020	0.00	1,264.51	0.00	0.00	0.00	1,342.91	26.86	1,316.05
2021	1,316.05	1,306.69	1.34	0.00	0.00	2,783.93	55.68	2,728.25
2022	2,728.25	1,350.92	4.06	0.00	0.00	4,327.75	86.56	4,241.20
2023	4,241.20	1,396.94	8.29	0.00	0.00	5,978.90	119.58	5,859.32
2024	5,859.32	1,444.05	14.26	0.00	0.00	7,741.04	154.82	7,586.22
2025	7,586.22	1,492.05	21.85	0.00	0.00	9,617.91	192.36	9,425.55
2026	9,425.55	1,544.03	31.25	0.00	0.00	11,616.51	232.33	11,384.17
2027	11,384.17	1,600.76	42.15	0.00	0.00	13,745.23	274.90	13,470.33
2028	13,470.33	1,658.26	55.03	0.00	0.00	16,006.13	320.16	15,687.96
2029	15,687.96	1,717.55	68.80	0.79	0.54	18,410.17	368.20	18,041.97
2030	18,041.97	1,778.91	82.29	2.36	1.68	20,958.10	419.16	20,538.94
2031	20,538.94	1,844.51	99.85	2.36	1.67	23,660.90	473.22	23,187.68
2032	23,187.68	1,913.96	114.82	4.82	3.40	26,527.27	530.55	25,996.72
2033	25,996.72	1,986.27	130.32	8.35	5.80	29,564.51	591.29	28,973.22
2034	28,973.22	2,058.80	147.96	12.80	8.88	32,775.84	655.52	32,120.33
2035	32,120.33	2,133.25	167.10	18.30	12.70	36,166.91	723.34	35,443.57
2036	35,443.57	2,213.18	186.34	24.93	16.89	39,749.17	794.98	38,954.18
2037	38,954.18	2,299.94	216.62	25.74	16.05	43,537.46	870.75	42,666.71
2038	42,666.71	2,391.54	236.46	33.94	20.61	47,542.82	950.86	46,591.96
2039	46,591.96	2,486.92	257.16	43.44	26.08	51,774.84	1,035.50	50,739.34
2040	50,739.34	2,586.43	279.78	54.01	31.57	56,243.96	1,124.88	55,119.08
2041	55,119.08	2,689.26	305.00	66.15	36.82	60,959.19	1,219.18	59,740.01

Table 3 – *Continued from previous page. . .*

Year	Beginning FAST Balance	Contribution	FAST Re-tirement Payout	FAST Residual Payout	Healthcare Loan Repayment	FAST Balance Plus 6.2% Growth	FAST Fee	Ending FAST Balance
2042	59,740.01	2,791.91	335.71	79.27	42.71	65,922.83	1,318.46	64,604.37
2043	64,604.37	2,902.70	388.44	82.15	39.73	71,150.56	1,423.01	69,727.55
2044	69,727.55	3,013.21	427.48	96.77	46.32	76,644.75	1,532.89	75,111.85
2045	75,111.85	3,125.31	470.98	114.12	53.91	82,409.24	1,648.18	80,761.05
2046	80,761.05	3,240.91	515.88	133.50	62.72	88,453.83	1,769.08	86,684.76
2047	86,684.76	3,361.41	565.26	156.67	69.32	94,788.73	1,895.77	92,892.96
2048	92,892.96	3,484.13	621.86	178.58	77.36	101,420.25	2,028.40	99,391.84
2049	99,391.84	3,610.03	714.77	183.79	71.92	108,357.33	2,167.15	106,190.19
2050	106,190.19	3,736.17	787.25	207.22	80.76	115,599.90	2,312.00	113,287.90
2051	113,287.90	3,873.81	859.43	233.78	89.51	123,169.70	2,463.39	120,706.31
2052	120,706.31	4,012.04	941.79	263.61	97.95	131,066.73	2,621.33	128,445.40
2053	128,445.40	4,152.55	1,030.51	298.21	105.52	139,295.86	2,785.92	136,509.94
2054	136,509.94	4,295.69	1,123.62	338.18	114.75	147,861.28	2,957.23	144,904.05
2055	144,904.05	4,439.57	1,283.45	346.36	106.17	156,759.32	3,135.19	153,624.13
2056	153,624.13	4,586.94	1,400.74	385.52	119.05	165,996.72	3,319.93	162,676.78
2057	162,676.78	4,745.27	1,518.17	433.88	130.26	175,590.80	3,511.82	172,078.99
2058	172,078.99	4,904.79	1,639.96	488.42	143.40	185,544.14	3,710.88	181,833.26
2059	181,833.26	5,077.33	1,757.59	546.43	157.65	195,884.75	3,917.70	191,967.06
2060	191,967.06	5,253.99	1,963.47	561.06	142.41	206,616.47	4,132.33	202,484.14
2061	202,484.14	5,437.93	2,101.79	622.06	159.59	217,751.01	4,355.02	213,395.99
2062	213,395.99	5,624.75	2,250.30	693.58	173.58	229,289.29	4,585.79	224,703.51
2063	224,703.51	5,819.16	2,409.77	769.09	189.63	241,237.73	4,824.75	236,412.98
2064	236,412.98	6,020.49	2,566.80	856.86	205.34	253,610.35	5,072.21	248,538.14
2065	248,538.14	6,230.05	2,744.06	947.18	221.20	266,408.81	5,328.18	261,080.63
2066	261,080.63	6,443.13	3,041.81	971.86	195.50	279,640.09	5,592.80	274,047.29
2067	274,047.29	6,661.70	3,230.86	1,069.94	216.50	293,315.58	5,866.31	287,449.27
2068	287,449.27	6,888.48	3,421.45	1,179.89	235.75	307,449.70	6,148.99	301,300.71
2069	301,300.71	7,123.42	3,614.93	1,299.79	256.30	322,054.80	6,441.10	315,613.71
2070	315,613.71	7,368.94	3,789.17	1,438.71	274.74	337,163.78	6,743.28	330,420.51
2071	330,420.51	7,621.54	3,985.86	1,590.05	290.54	352,770.49	7,055.41	345,715.08
2072	345,715.08	7,871.60	4,376.31	1,625.34	253.61	368,865.97	7,377.32	361,488.65
2073	361,488.65	8,134.91	4,590.02	1,767.84	285.66	385,484.80	7,709.70	377,775.11
2074	377,775.11	8,406.07	4,804.10	1,937.84	302.50	402,643.21	8,052.86	394,590.35

Table 3 – *Continued from previous page...*

Year	Beginning FAST Balance	Contribution	FAST Retirement Payout	FAST Residual Payout	Healthcare Loan Repayment	FAST Balance Plus 6.2% Growth	FAST Fee	Ending FAST Balance
2075	394,590.35	8,706.54	5,002.71	2,111.14	316.48	420,410.29	8,408.21	412,002.08
2076	412,002.08	9,016.20	5,199.54	2,299.07	330.97	438,806.40	8,776.13	430,030.27
2077	430,030.27	9,333.25	5,399.45	2,499.47	344.08	457,849.98	9,157.00	448,692.98
2078	448,692.98	9,664.06	5,829.90	2,555.95	285.13	477,566.60	9,551.33	468,015.27
2079	468,015.27	10,003.28	6,038.65	2,751.39	320.25	497,980.57	9,959.61	488,020.96
2080	488,020.96	10,351.42	6,246.10	2,976.04	342.96	519,113.33	10,382.27	508,731.06
2081	508,731.06	10,710.95	6,466.09	3,213.20	362.47	540,983.06	10,819.66	530,163.40
2082	530,163.40	11,092.67	6,678.20	3,476.06	378.90	563,627.73	11,272.55	552,355.18
2083	552,355.18	11,480.47	6,900.58	3,763.90	383.42	587,060.59	11,741.21	575,319.37
2084	575,319.37	11,873.83	7,438.06	3,829.42	314.29	611,299.33	12,225.99	599,073.35
2085	599,073.35	12,288.18	7,687.61	4,102.69	344.35	636,378.95	12,727.58	623,651.37
2086	623,651.37	12,716.36	7,944.25	4,400.92	360.94	662,328.64	13,246.57	649,082.07
2087	649,082.07	13,163.54	8,200.97	4,723.19	367.41	689,189.19	13,783.78	675,405.40
2088	675,405.40	13,606.89	8,508.54	5,044.26	372.79	716,942.08	14,338.84	702,603.23
2089	702,603.23	14,078.47	9,155.48	5,109.47	302.86	745,644.95	14,912.90	730,732.05
2090	730,732.05	14,568.67	9,466.87	5,438.20	331.99	775,327.61	15,506.55	759,821.05
2091	759,821.05	15,080.36	9,763.94	5,810.04	342.58	806,041.92	16,120.84	789,921.08
2092	789,921.08	15,606.94	10,094.65	6,186.42	348.00	837,810.57	16,756.21	821,054.36
2093	821,054.36	16,152.36	10,426.94	6,589.48	339.37	870,681.69	17,413.63	853,268.06
2094	853,268.06	16,722.00	10,784.37	6,970.51	337.89	904,714.91	18,094.30	886,620.62
2095	886,620.62	17,316.26	11,550.52	7,031.04	271.00	939,959.54	18,799.19	921,160.35
2096	921,160.35	17,916.75	11,978.50	7,403.73	290.67	976,407.25	19,528.14	956,879.10
2097	956,879.10	18,542.78	12,415.73	7,802.97	297.73	1,014,109.59	20,282.19	993,827.40
2098	993,827.40	19,189.06	12,854.54	8,221.51	299.77	1,053,122.37	21,062.45	1,032,059.92
2099	1,032,059.92	19,866.08	13,305.09	8,654.81	298.19	1,093,507.32	21,870.15	1,071,637.17
2100	1,071,637.17	20,568.52	13,777.01	9,107.49	292.47	1,135,308.50	22,706.17	1,112,602.33

Table 4: *PFA Borrowing Assuming 6.2% Market Return*

This table contains the projected borrowing PFA will require in order to cover the Social Security guarantee and to make the healthcare loans "Year" indicates the year to which the data correspond. "Ending FAST Balance" is the market value of the FAST accounts at the end of the year "FAST Fee" is the annual 2% management fee. "Social Security Commitment Net FAST" is the difference between the amount retirees would have earned under Social Security and the cash flows produced by PFA. "New Healthcare Borrowing" is the new amount borrowed each year in the form of healthcare loans by plan participants. "Total Annual PFA Related Borrowing" is the annual Social Security shortfall plus the healthcare loan borrowing. "Total Annual PFA Related Borrowing Net FAST Fee" is the annual Social Security shortfall plus the healthcare loan borrowing minus the PFA fee. "Cumulative Net FAST Borrowing" is the aggregate borrowing necessary to finance PFA. See page 4 for a discussion on the jagged nature of these projections. All values are reported in billions of dollars.

Year	Ending FAST Balance	FAST Fee	Social Security Commitment Net FAST	New Healthcare Borrowing	Total Annual PFA Borrowing	Total Annual PFA Borrowing Net FAST Fee	Cumulative Net FAST Borrowing
2020	1,316.05	26.86	1,082.90	875.51	1,958.41	1,931.55	1,931.55
2021	2,728.25	55.68	1,148.66	855.17	2,003.83	1,948.15	3,879.70
2022	4,241.20	86.56	1,411.04	820.31	2,231.35	2,144.79	6,024.49
2023	5,859.32	119.58	1,406.81	804.42	2,211.23	2,091.65	8,116.14
2024	7,586.22	154.82	1,400.84	784.99	2,185.83	2,031.01	10,147.15
2025	9,425.55	192.36	1,393.25	760.92	2,154.17	1,961.81	12,108.96
2026	11,384.17	232.33	1,824.75	732.31	2,557.06	2,324.73	14,433.69
2027	13,470.33	274.90	1,813.85	719.09	2,532.94	2,258.04	16,691.73
2028	15,687.96	320.16	1,800.97	686.43	2,487.40	2,167.24	18,858.97
2029	18,041.97	368.20	1,786.41	671.50	2,457.91	2,089.71	20,948.68
2030	20,538.94	419.16	1,770.59	651.79	2,423.14	2,003.98	22,952.66
2031	23,187.68	473.22	2,753.16	627.21	3,397.80	2,924.58	25,877.24
2032	25,996.72	530.55	2,734.13	611.57	3,364.73	2,834.18	28,711.42
2033	28,973.22	591.29	2,712.04	583.96	3,318.09	2,726.80	31,438.22
2034	32,120.33	655.52	2,687.40	555.00	3,267.04	2,611.52	34,049.74
2035	35,443.57	723.34	2,661.53	533.43	3,220.83	2,497.49	36,547.23
2036	38,954.18	794.98	2,630.44	515.15	3,176.68	2,381.70	38,928.93
2037	42,666.71	870.75	2,602.40	504.06	3,134.50	2,263.75	41,192.68
2038	46,591.96	950.86	2,572.20	488.71	3,091.11	2,140.25	43,332.93
2039	50,739.34	1,035.50	2,539.01	453.42	3,025.62	1,990.12	45,323.05
2040	55,119.08	1,124.88	3,776.05	433.25	2,972.26	1,847.38	47,170.43
2041	59,740.01	1,219.18		412.25	4,188.30	2,969.12	50,139.55

149

Table 4 – Continued from previous page...

Year	Ending FAST Balance	FAST Fee	Social Security Commitment Net FAST	New Healthcare Borrowing	Total Annual PFA Borrowing	Total Annual PFA Borrowing Net FAST Fee	Cumulative Net FAST Borrowing
2042	64,604.37	1,318.46	3,732.22	397.00	4,129.22	2,810.76	52,950.31
2043	69,727.55	1,423.01	3,676.61	387.80	4,064.41	2,641.40	55,591.71
2044	75,111.85	1,532.89	3,622.95	372.16	3,995.11	2,462.22	58,053.93
2045	80,761.05	1,648.18	3,562.10	348.11	3,910.21	2,262.03	60,315.96
2046	86,684.76	1,769.08	3,497.82	316.41	3,814.23	2,045.15	62,361.11
2047	92,892.96	1,895.77	3,425.27	298.42	3,723.69	1,827.92	64,189.03
2048	99,391.84	2,028.40	3,346.76	276.26	3,623.02	1,594.62	65,783.65
2049	106,190.19	2,167.15	3,248.64	270.86	3,519.50	1,352.35	67,136.00
2050	113,287.90	2,312.00	3,152.73	252.50	3,405.23	1,093.23	68,229.23
2051	120,706.31	2,463.39	3,201.19	230.99	3,432.18	968.79	69,198.02
2052	128,445.40	2,621.33	3,242.60	211.44	3,454.04	832.71	70,030.73
2053	136,509.94	2,785.92	3,279.28	193.55	3,472.83	686.91	70,717.64
2054	144,904.05	2,957.23	3,306.20	173.68	3,479.88	522.65	71,240.29
2055	153,624.13	3,135.19	3,304.59	174.21	3,478.80	343.61	71,583.90
2056	162,676.78	3,319.93	3,320.94	152.38	3,473.32	153.39	71,737.29
2057	172,078.99	3,511.82	3,334.35	133.50	3,467.85	-43.97	71,693.32
2058	181,833.26	3,710.88	3,343.62	114.90	3,458.52	-252.36	71,440.96
2059	191,967.06	3,917.70	3,359.98	94.79	3,454.77	-462.93	70,978.03
2060	202,484.14	4,132.33	3,337.87	98.89	3,436.76	-695.57	70,282.46
2061	213,395.99	4,355.02	3,343.35	73.14	3,416.49	-938.53	69,343.93
2062	224,703.51	4,585.79	3,334.52	50.44	3,384.96	-1,200.83	68,143.10
2063	236,412.98	4,824.75	3,323.54	29.88	3,353.42	-1,471.33	66,671.77
2064	248,538.14	5,072.21	3,309.14	8.13	3,317.27	-1,754.94	64,916.83
2065	261,080.63	5,328.18	3,278.36	-13.08	3,265.28	-2,062.90	62,853.93
2066	274,047.29	5,592.80	3,199.13	7.18	3,206.31	-2,386.49	60,467.44
2067	287,449.27	5,866.31	3,168.00	-19.78	3,148.22	-2,718.09	57,749.35
2068	301,300.71	6,148.99	3,129.86	-44.77	3,085.09	-3,063.90	54,685.45
2069	315,613.71	6,441.10	3,091.68	-72.29	3,019.39	-3,421.71	51,263.74
2070	330,420.51	6,743.28	3,060.12	-95.21	2,964.91	-3,778.37	47,485.37
2071	345,715.08	7,055.41	3,006.49	-114.78	2,891.71	-4,163.70	43,321.67
2072	361,488.65	7,377.32	2,881.55	-83.74	2,797.81	-4,579.51	38,742.16
2073	377,775.11	7,709.70	2,838.94	-121.05	2,717.89	-4,991.81	33,750.35

Table 4 – *Continued from previous page…*

Year	Ending FAST Balance	FAST Fee	Social Security Commitment Net FAST	New Healthcare Borrowing	Total Annual PFA Borrowing	Total Annual PFA Borrowing Net FAST Fee	Cumulative Net FAST Borrowing
2074	394,590.35	8,052.86	2,781.26	-142.93	2,638.33	-5,414.53	28,335.82
2075	412,002.08	8,408.21	2,748.55	-162.12	2,586.43	-5,821.78	22,514.04
2076	430,030.27	8,776.13	2,709.39	-180.43	2,528.96	-6,247.17	16,266.87
2077	448,692.98	9,157.00	2,667.48	-198.32	2,469.16	-6,687.84	9,579.03
2078	468,015.27	9,551.33	2,551.75	-142.37	2,409.38	-7,141.95	2,437.08
2079	488,020.96	9,959.61	2,531.56	-179.58	2,351.98	-7,607.63	-5,170.55
2080	508,731.06	10,382.27	2,496.26	-204.90	2,291.36	-8,090.91	-13,261.46
2081	530,163.40	10,819.66	2,455.11	-228.44	2,226.67	-8,592.99	-21,854.45
2082	552,355.18	11,272.55	2,408.94	-248.80	2,160.14	-9,112.41	-30,966.86
2083	575,319.37	11,741.21	2,340.32	-257.30	2,083.02	-9,658.19	-40,625.05
2084	599,073.35	12,225.99	2,198.12	-191.69	2,006.43	-10,219.56	-50,844.61
2085	623,651.37	12,727.58	2,148.90	-224.56	1,924.34	-10,803.24	-61,647.85
2086	649,082.07	13,246.57	2,086.83	-242.57	1,844.26	-11,402.31	-73,050.16
2087	675,405.40	13,783.78	2,019.84	-250.11	1,769.73	-12,014.05	-85,064.21
2088	702,603.23	14,338.84	1,916.00	-257.66	1,658.34	-12,680.50	-97,744.71
2089	730,732.05	14,912.90	1,747.85	-191.86	1,555.99	-13,356.91	-111,101.62
2090	759,821.05	15,506.55	1,670.93	-226.04	1,444.89	-14,061.66	-125,163.28
2091	789,921.08	16,120.84	1,584.42	-240.34	1,344.08	-14,776.76	-139,940.04
2092	821,054.36	16,756.21	1,485.33	-245.49	1,239.84	-15,516.37	-155,456.41
2093	853,268.06	17,413.63	1,377.18	-236.20	1,140.98	-16,272.65	-171,729.06
2094	886,620.62	18,094.30	1,285.12	-237.13	1,047.99	-17,046.31	-188,775.37
2095	921,160.35	18,799.19	1,130.44	-174.03	956.41	-17,842.78	-206,618.15
2096	956,879.10	19,528.14	1,027.37	-198.92	828.45	-18,699.69	-225,317.84
2097	993,827.40	20,282.19	914.10	-209.58	704.52	-19,577.67	-244,895.51
2098	1,032,059.92	21,062.45	805.55	-212.67	592.88	-20,469.57	-265,365.08
2099	1,071,637.17	21,870.15	696.10	-210.90	485.20	-21,384.95	-286,750.03
2100	1,112,602.33	22,706.17	571.50	-205.01	366.49	-22,339.68	-309,089.71

Evaluating the Feasibility of Plan For America[1]

Table 5: *PFA Impact on the Government Assuming 6.2% Market Return*

This table contains the projected PFA impact on the Federal Government of the United State of America. "Year" indicates the year to which the data correspond. "Federal Deficit" is the projected Federal Deficit under current environment. "Total Federal Surplus (PFA)" represents the amount of surplus the Federal Government would run if PFA were enacted and fully implemented, including interest on any debt issued to support PFA and benefit once the FAST Fee can be distributed to the government. "Total Federal Surplus (PFA with Excess FAST Fee)" represents the Federal Surplus when the FAST Fee is applied back to the Federal Government budget after it has completely covered all borrowing of the plan. "Federal Debt Held by the Public" is the amount of debt the Federal Government is expected to carry under the current environment. "FAST Fee" is the annual 2% management fee. "Total PFA Borrowing Net Fast Fee" is the amount of PFA borrowing that would need to be funded by outside sources after using the Fast fee as a source of capital. See page 4 for a discussion on the jagged nature of these projections. All values are reported in billions of dollars.

Year	Total Federal Deficit	Federal Debt Held by the Public	Total Federal Surplus (PFA)	Total Federal Surplus (PFA with Excess FAST Fee)	FAST Fee	Total PFA Borrowing Net FAST Fee
2020	1,000.00	17,900.00	-27.60	-27.60	26.86	1,931.55
2021	1,000.00	18,900.00	35.00	35.00	55.68	3,879.70
2022	1,100.00	20,100.00	288.40	288.40	86.56	6,024.49
2023	1,100.00	21,200.00	288.40	288.40	119.58	8,116.14
2024	1,200.00	22,500.00	188.40	188.40	154.82	10,147.15
2025	1,300.00	23,800.00	88.40	88.40	192.36	12,108.96
2026	1,300.00	25,200.00	780.00	780.00	232.33	14,433.69
2027	1,300.00	26,500.00	780.00	780.00	274.90	16,691.73
2028	1,500.00	28,200.00	580.00	580.00	320.16	18,858.97
2029	1,500.00	29,700.00	580.00	580.00	368.20	20,948.68
2030	1,700.00	31,400.00	380.00	380.00	419.16	22,952.66
2031	1,900.00	33,400.00	1,839.20	1,839.20	473.22	25,877.24
2032	2,100.00	35,500.00	1,639.20	1,639.20	530.55	28,711.42
2033	2,200.00	37,700.00	1,539.20	1,539.20	591.29	31,438.22
2034	2,400.00	40,200.00	1,339.20	1,339.20	655.52	34,049.74
2035	2,600.00	42,800.00	1,139.20	1,139.20	723.34	36,547.23
2036	2,800.00	45,700.00	939.20	939.20	794.98	38,928.93
2037	3,100.00	48,700.00	639.20	639.20	870.75	41,192.68
2038	3,300.00	52,000.00	439.20	439.20	950.86	43,332.93
2039	3,600.00	55,600.00	139.20	139.20	1,035.50	45,323.05
2040	3,800.00	59,400.00	-60.80	-60.80	1,124.88	47,170.43
2041	4,100.00	63,500.00	2,120.80	2,120.80	1,219.18	50,139.55
2042	4,400.00	67,900.00	1,820.80	1,820.80	1,318.46	52,950.31
2043	4,700.00	72,700.00	1,520.80	1,520.80	1,423.01	55,591.71
2044	5,100.00	77,700.00	1,120.80	1,120.80	1,532.89	58,053.93
2045	5,400.00	83,100.00	820.80	820.80	1,648.18	60,315.96
2046	5,800.00	89,000.00	420.80	420.80	1,769.08	62,361.11
2047	6,200.00	95,200.00	20.80	20.80	1,895.77	64,189.03
2048	6,700.00	101,800.00	-479.20	-479.20	2,028.40	65,783.65
2049	7,100.00	109,000.00	-879.20	-879.20	2,167.15	67,136.00
2050	7,700.00	116,600.00	-1,479.20	-1,479.20	2,312.00	68,229.23

Evaluating the Feasibility of Plan For America[1]

Table 5 – *Continued from previous page...*

Year	Total Federal Deficit	Federal Debt Held by the Public	Total Federal Surplus (PFA)	Total Federal Surplus (PFA with Excess FAST Fee)	FAST Fee	Total PFA Borrowing Net FAST Fee
2051	7,929.60	120,960.00	-1,488.00	-1,488.00	2,463.39	69,198.02
2052	8,224.60	125,460.00	-1,552.60	-1,552.60	2,621.33	70,030.73
2053	8,519.60	129,960.00	-1,607.60	-1,607.60	2,785.92	70,717.64
2054	8,826.40	134,640.00	-1,674.40	-1,674.40	2,957.23	71,240.29
2055	9,145.00	139,500.00	-1,743.40	-1,743.40	3,135.19	71,583.90
2056	9,475.40	144,540.00	-1,814.60	-1,814.60	3,319.93	71,737.29
2057	9,817.60	149,760.00	-1,888.00	-1,888.00	3,511.82	71,693.32
2058	10,171.60	155,160.00	-1,963.60	-1,963.60	3,710.88	71,440.96
2059	10,537.40	160,740.00	-2,041.40	-2,041.40	3,917.70	70,978.03
2060	10,926.80	166,680.00	-2,133.20	-2,133.20	4,132.33	70,282.46
2061	11,328.00	172,800.00	-2,227.20	-2,227.20	4,355.02	69,343.93
2062	11,741.00	179,100.00	-2,323.40	-2,323.40	4,585.79	68,143.10
2063	12,165.80	185,580.00	-2,412.20	-2,412.20	4,824.75	66,671.77
2064	12,614.20	192,420.00	-2,515.00	-2,515.00	5,072.21	64,916.83
2065	13,074.40	199,440.00	-2,620.00	-2,620.00	5,328.18	62,853.93
2066	13,546.40	206,640.00	-2,727.20	-2,727.20	5,592.80	60,467.44
2067	14,042.00	214,200.00	-2,838.80	-2,838.80	5,866.31	57,749.35
2068	14,549.40	221,940.00	-2,952.60	-2,952.60	6,148.99	54,685.45
2069	15,080.40	230,040.00	-3,070.80	-3,070.80	6,441.10	51,263.74
2070	15,635.00	238,500.00	-3,203.00	-3,203.00	6,743.28	47,485.37
2071	16,201.40	247,140.00	-3,327.80	-3,327.80	7,055.41	43,321.67
2072	16,791.40	256,140.00	-3,466.60	-3,466.60	7,377.32	38,742.16
2073	17,405.00	265,500.00	-3,609.80	-3,609.80	7,709.70	33,750.35
2074	18,042.20	275,220.00	-3,757.40	-3,757.40	8,052.86	28,335.82
2075	18,703.00	285,300.00	-3,909.40	-3,909.40	8,408.21	22,514.04
2076	19,387.40	295,740.00	-4,075.40	-4,075.40	8,776.13	16,266.87
2077	20,095.40	306,540.00	-4,245.80	-4,245.80	9,157.00	9,579.03
2078	20,827.00	317,700.00	-4,420.60	-4,420.60	9,551.33	2,437.08
2079	21,582.20	329,220.00	-4,599.80	5,359.81	9,959.61	-5,170.55
2080	22,372.80	341,280.00	-4,795.20	5,587.07	10,382.27	-13,261.46
2081	23,187.00	353,700.00	-4,985.40	5,834.26	10,819.66	-21,854.45
2082	24,036.60	366,660.00	-5,191.80	6,080.75	11,272.55	-30,966.86
2083	24,909.80	379,980.00	-5,402.60	6,338.61	11,741.21	-40,625.05
2084	25,818.40	393,840.00	-5,620.00	6,605.99	12,225.99	-50,844.61
2085	26,762.40	408,240.00	-5,853.60	6,873.98	12,727.58	-61,647.85
2086	27,741.80	423,180.00	-6,093.80	7,152.77	13,246.57	-73,050.16
2087	28,756.60	438,660.00	-6,340.60	7,443.18	13,783.78	-85,064.21
2088	29,806.80	454,680.00	-6,603.60	7,735.24	14,338.84	-97,744.71
2089	30,892.40	471,240.00	-6,873.20	8,039.70	14,912.90	-111,101.62
2090	32,025.20	488,520.00	-7,161.20	8,345.35	15,506.55	-125,163.28
2091	33,193.40	506,340.00	-7,455.80	8,665.04	16,120.84	-139,940.04
2092	34,408.80	524,880.00	-7,759.20	8,997.01	16,756.21	-155,456.41
2093	35,659.60	543,960.00	-8,069.20	9,344.43	17,413.63	-171,729.06

Table 5 – *Continued from previous page...*

Year	Total Federal Deficit	Federal Debt Held by the Public	Total Federal Surplus (PFA)	Total Federal Surplus (PFA with Excess FAST Fee)	FAST Fee	Total PFA Borrowing Net FAST Fee
2094	36,957.60	563,760.00	-8,397.60	9,696.70	18,094.30	-188,775.37
2095	38,302.80	584,280.00	-8,734.80	10,064.39	18,799.19	-206,618.15
2096	39,707.00	605,700.00	-9,092.60	10,435.54	19,528.14	-225,317.84
2097	41,158.40	627,840.00	-9,459.20	10,822.99	20,282.19	-244,895.51
2098	42,657.00	650,700.00	-9,834.60	11,227.85	21,062.45	-265,365.08
2099	44,214.60	674,460.00	-10,230.60	11,639.55	21,870.15	-286,750.03
2100	45,831.20	699,120.00	-10,647.20	12,058.97	22,706.17	-309,089.71

Table 6: *PFA Cash Flows Assuming 10.2% Market Return*

This table contains the projected PFA cash flows under the base case scenario considered in this paper. Reading across the table you can follow the life cycle of the aggregate FAST accounts just as is described in section 2. "Year" indicates the year to which the data correspond. "Beginning FAST Balance" is the aggregate balance of all FAST accounts at the beginning of the year. "Contribution" is the amount FAST participants contribute to their accounts, which is 15.3% of their wages. "FAST Retirement Payout" is the amount that gets paid out to the designated beneficiaries after the original account holder has passed. "Healthcare Loan Repayment" is the amount paid toward outstanding healthcare loans by plan participants. "FAST Balance Plus 10.2% Growth" is the account value after combining the beginning balance with the contribution and allowing it to grow at 10.2%. "FAST Fee" is the annual 2% management fee. "Ending FAST Balance" is the market value of the FAST accounts at the end of the year. See page 4 for a discussion on the jagged nature of these projections. All values are reported in billions of dollars.

Year	Beginning FAST Balance	Contribution	FAST Retirement Payout	Healthcare Loan Repayment	FAST Residual Payout	FAST Balance Plus 10.2% Growth	FAST Fee	Ending FAST Balance
2020	0.00	1,264.51	0.00	0.00	0.00	1,393.49	27.87	1,365.62
2021	1,365.62	1,306.69	1.39	0.00	0.00	2,943.35	58.87	2,884.48
2022	2,884.48	1,350.92	4.32	0.00	0.00	4,662.65	93.25	4,569.39
2023	4,569.39	1,396.94	9.04	0.00	0.00	6,564.94	131.30	6,433.64
2024	6,433.64	1,444.05	15.93	0.00	0.00	8,663.66	173.27	8,490.38
2025	8,490.38	1,492.05	25.03	0.00	0.00	10,973.05	219.46	10,753.59
2026	10,753.59	1,544.03	36.70	0.00	0.00	13,511.54	270.23	13,241.31
2027	13,241.31	1,600.76	50.76	0.00	0.00	16,300.01	326.00	15,974.01
2028	15,974.01	1,658.26	67.95	0.00	0.00	19,355.89	387.12	18,968.77
2029	18,968.77	1,717.55	86.93	0.75	1.10	22,698.49	453.97	22,244.52
2030	22,244.52	1,778.91	106.34	2.40	3.38	26,350.27	527.01	25,823.26
2031	25,823.26	1,844.51	132.46	2.48	3.50	30,337.32	606.75	29,730.57
2032	29,730.57	1,913.96	155.77	5.14	7.36	34,686.83	693.74	33,993.09
2033	33,993.09	1,986.27	180.65	8.97	13.08	39,425.88	788.52	38,637.37
2034	38,637.37	2,058.80	209.38	13.92	20.73	44,578.26	891.57	43,686.70
2035	43,686.70	2,133.25	241.31	19.66	31.12	50,171.70	1,003.43	49,168.26
2036	49,168.26	2,213.18	274.75	26.70	43.55	56,242.16	1,124.84	55,117.32
2037	55,117.32	2,299.94	328.23	25.87	46.96	62,831.86	1,256.64	61,575.22
2038	61,575.22	2,391.54	366.08	33.80	63.69	69,980.52	1,399.61	68,580.91
2039	68,580.91	2,486.92	406.62	42.82	84.56	77,728.28	1,554.57	76,173.71
2040	76,173.71	2,586.43	451.93	52.70	108.16	86,118.38	1,722.37	84,396.01

Table 6 – *Continued from previous page. . .*

Year	Beginning FAST Balance	Contribu- tion	FAST Re- tirement Payout	Health- care Loan Repay- ment	FAST Residual Payout	FAST Balance Plus 10.2% Growth	FAST Fee	Ending FAST Balance
2041	84,396.01	2,689.26	503.29	61.99	136.64	95,194.45	1,903.89	93,290.56
2042	93,290.56	2,791.91	565.65	73.28	168.16	104,993.47	2,099.87	102,893.60
2043	102,893.60	2,902.70	672.34	68.29	182.03	115,570.75	2,311.42	113,259.34
2044	113,259.34	3,013.21	755.57	82.34	219.18	126,967.43	2,539.35	124,428.08
2045	124,428.08	3,125.31	849.67	96.07	266.93	139,227.48	2,784.55	136,442.93
2046	136,442.93	3,240.91	950.21	112.35	322.15	152,405.65	3,048.11	149,357.53
2047	149,357.53	3,361.41	1,063.59	126.55	386.65	166,558.66	3,331.17	163,227.49
2048	163,227.49	3,484.13	1,196.09	141.36	455.23	181,740.67	3,634.81	178,105.86
2049	178,105.86	3,610.03	1,413.09	130.82	487.70	198,012.07	3,960.24	194,051.83
2050	194,051.83	3,736.17	1,591.37	147.54	567.38	215,420.84	4,308.42	211,112.43
2051	211,112.43	3,873.81	1,777.63	163.18	660.38	234,048.33	4,680.97	229,367.37
2052	229,367.37	4,012.04	1,993.02	179.18	765.88	253,946.34	5,078.93	248,867.42
2053	248,867.42	4,152.55	2,231.54	192.83	889.69	275,175.91	5,503.52	269,672.39
2054	269,672.39	4,295.69	2,489.38	208.32	1,036.39	297,797.85	5,955.96	291,841.89
2055	291,841.89	4,439.57	2,922.86	178.93	1,111.54	321,859.09	6,437.18	315,421.91
2056	315,421.91	4,586.94	3,264.92	202.87	1,272.39	347,426.07	6,948.52	340,477.55
2057	340,477.55	4,745.27	3,622.55	220.43	1,469.77	374,580.89	7,491.62	367,089.28
2058	367,089.28	4,904.79	4,005.82	240.80	1,698.15	403,386.33	8,067.73	395,318.60
2059	395,318.60	5,077.33	4,397.96	263.48	1,950.55	433,949.90	8,679.00	425,270.90
2060	425,270.90	5,253.99	5,056.49	213.60	2,081.82	466,336.63	9,326.73	457,009.90
2061	457,009.90	5,437.93	5,545.39	249.92	2,363.91	500,626.04	10,012.52	490,613.52
2062	490,613.52	5,624.75	6,082.21	273.96	2,697.75	536,877.16	10,737.54	526,139.62
2063	526,139.62	5,819.16	6,672.85	295.13	3,072.66	575,153.79	11,503.08	563,650.72
2064	563,650.72	6,020.49	7,282.35	314.17	3,508.96	615,539.44	12,310.79	603,228.65
2065	603,228.65	6,230.05	7,977.61	338.42	3,973.55	658,080.36	13,161.61	644,918.75
2066	644,918.75	6,443.13	9,083.37	257.43	4,213.06	702,864.44	14,057.29	688,807.16
2067	688,807.16	6,661.70	9,846.65	310.61	4,738.87	749,991.14	14,999.82	734,991.32
2068	734,991.32	6,888.48	10,624.44	342.30	5,353.36	799,566.78	15,991.34	783,575.45
2069	783,575.45	7,123.42	11,417.87	374.60	6,042.95	851,695.52	17,033.91	834,661.61
2070	834,661.61	7,368.94	12,159.77	395.39	6,845.79	906,537.83	18,130.76	888,407.07
2071	888,407.07	7,621.54	12,965.37	414.80	7,731.83	964,158.11	19,283.16	944,874.95
2072	944,874.95	7,871.60	14,508.36	284.03	8,162.09	1,024,630.86	20,492.62	1,004,138.25

156

Table 6 – *Continued from previous page. . .*

Year	Beginning FAST Balance	Contribution	FAST Retirement Payout	Healthcare Loan Repayment	FAST Residual Payout	FAST Balance Plus 10.2% Growth	FAST Fee	Ending FAST Balance
2073	1,004,138.25	8,134.91	15,397.78	370.87	9,095.48	1,088,124.75	21,762.50	1,066,362.26
2074	1,066,362.26	8,406.07	16,286.66	403.49	10,188.97	1,154,773.90	23,095.48	1,131,678.42
2075	1,131,678.42	8,706.54	17,147.11	428.23	11,353.12	1,224,825.07	24,496.50	1,200,328.57
2076	1,200,328.57	9,016.20	17,990.50	432.29	12,667.44	1,298,436.50	25,968.73	1,272,467.77
2077	1,272,467.77	9,333.25	18,832.56	451.28	14,086.94	1,375,770.12	27,515.40	1,348,254.72
2078	1,348,254.72	9,664.06	20,702.84	276.12	14,796.54	1,457,001.89	29,140.04	1,427,861.85
2079	1,427,861.85	10,003.28	21,574.91	392.28	16,333.18	1,542,320.38	30,846.41	1,511,473.97
2080	1,511,473.97	10,351.42	22,412.77	437.29	18,110.94	1,631,912.56	32,638.25	1,599,274.30
2081	1,599,274.30	10,710.95	23,264.35	465.39	20,049.95	1,725,958.53	34,519.17	1,691,439.36
2082	1,691,439.36	11,092.67	24,040.23	488.12	22,214.64	1,824,679.52	36,493.59	1,788,185.93
2083	1,788,185.93	11,480.47	24,841.35	481.27	24,556.99	1,928,265.04	38,565.30	1,889,699.74
2084	1,889,699.74	11,873.83	27,225.81	262.00	25,696.71	2,036,924.72	40,738.49	1,996,186.23
2085	1,996,186.23	12,288.18	28,134.14	409.98	28,119.50	2,150,895.50	43,017.91	2,107,877.59
2086	2,107,877.59	12,716.36	29,065.57	432.31	30,824.39	2,270,419.40	45,408.39	2,225,011.01
2087	2,225,011.01	13,163.54	29,995.74	439.71	33,719.17	2,395,769.97	47,915.40	2,347,854.57
2088	2,347,854.57	13,606.89	31,103.47	438.42	36,718.78	2,527,107.26	50,542.15	2,476,565.11
2089	2,476,565.11	14,078.47	34,018.24	235.02	38,288.15	2,664,748.59	53,294.97	2,611,453.62
2090	2,611,453.62	14,568.67	35,133.45	371.25	41,549.45	2,808,962.88	56,179.26	2,752,783.62
2091	2,752,783.62	15,080.36	36,182.97	394.64	45,184.55	2,960,084.21	59,201.68	2,900,882.53
2092	2,900,882.53	15,606.94	37,363.38	396.80	48,974.25	3,118,390.05	62,367.80	3,056,022.24
2093	3,056,022.24	16,152.36	38,557.04	395.64	52,976.46	3,284,230.50	65,684.61	3,218,545.89
2094	3,218,545.89	16,722.00	39,903.23	385.32	57,056.00	3,457,991.53	69,159.83	3,388,831.70
2095	3,388,831.70	17,316.26	43,469.58	205.07	59,347.88	3,640,044.22	72,800.88	3,567,243.34
2096	3,567,243.34	17,916.75	45,071.69	313.59	63,689.65	3,830,645.84	76,612.92	3,754,032.92
2097	3,754,032.92	18,542.78	46,716.48	326.00	68,372.04	4,030,191.62	80,603.83	3,949,587.79
2098	3,949,587.79	19,189.06	48,383.62	321.43	73,327.05	4,239,112.71	84,782.25	4,154,330.46
2099	4,154,330.46	19,866.08	50,110.73	311.61	78,534.63	4,457,854.01	89,157.08	4,368,696.93
2100	4,368,696.93	20,568.52	51,914.03	305.22	84,018.27	4,686,836.77	93,736.74	4,593,100.04

Table 7: *PFA Borrowing Assuming 10.2% Market Return*

This table contains the projected borrowing PFA will require in order to cover the Social Security guarantee and to make the healthcare loans. "Year" indicates the year to which the data correspond. "Ending FAST Balance" is the market value of the FAST accounts at the end of the year. "FAST Fee" is the annual 2% management fee. "Social Security Commitment Net FAST" is the difference between the amount retirees would have earned under Social Security and the cash flows produced by PFA. "New Healthcare Borrowing" is the new amount borrowed each year in the form of healthcare loans by plan participants. "Total Annual PFA Related Borrowing" is the annual Social Security shortfall plus the healthcare loan borrowing. "Total Annual PFA Related Borrowing Net FAST Fee" is the annual Social Security shortfall plus the healthcare loan borrowing minus the PFA fee. "Cumulative Net FAST Borrowing" is the aggregate borrowing necessary to finance PFA. See page 4 for a discussion on the jagged nature of these projections. All values are reported in billions of dollars.

Year	Ending FAST Balance	FAST Fee	Social Security Commitment Net FAST	New Healthcare Borrowing	Total Annual PFA Borrowing	Total Annual PFA Borrowing Net FAST Fee	Cumulative Net FAST Borrowing
2020	1,365.62	27.87	1,082.90	875.51	1,958.41	1,930.54	1,930.54
2021	2,884.48	58.87	1,148.61	855.17	2,003.78	1,944.91	3,875.45
2022	4,569.39	93.25	1,410.78	820.31	2,231.09	2,137.84	6,013.29
2023	6,433.64	131.30	1,406.06	804.42	2,210.48	2,079.18	8,092.47
2024	8,490.38	173.27	1,399.17	784.99	2,184.16	2,010.89	10,103.36
2025	10,753.59	219.46	1,390.07	760.92	2,150.99	1,931.53	12,034.89
2026	13,241.31	270.23	1,819.30	732.31	2,551.61	2,281.38	14,316.27
2027	15,974.01	326.00	1,805.24	719.09	2,524.33	2,198.33	16,514.60
2028	18,968.77	387.12	1,788.05	686.43	2,474.48	2,087.36	18,601.96
2029	22,244.52	453.97	1,767.97	671.28	2,439.25	1,985.28	20,587.24
2030	25,823.26	527.01	1,746.28	651.08	2,397.36	1,870.35	22,457.59
2031	29,730.57	606.75	2,736.84	626.40	3,363.24	2,756.49	25,214.08
2032	33,993.09	693.74	2,709.67	609.83	3,319.50	2,625.76	27,839.84
2033	38,637.37	788.52	2,679.07	580.79	3,259.86	2,471.34	30,311.18
2034	43,686.70	891.57	2,642.69	549.97	3,192.66	2,301.09	32,612.27
2035	49,168.26	1,003.43	2,600.37	526.47	3,126.84	2,123.41	34,735.68
2036	55,117.32	1,124.84	2,554.50	505.34	3,059.84	1,935.00	36,670.68
2037	61,575.22	1,256.64	2,497.61	494.24	2,991.85	1,735.21	38,405.89
2038	68,580.91	1,399.61	2,443.03	475.51	2,918.54	1,518.93	39,924.82
2039	76,173.71	1,554.57	2,381.62	436.68	2,818.30	1,263.73	41,188.55
2040	84,396.01	1,722.37	2,312.71	412.12	2,724.83	1,002.46	42,191.01
2041	93,290.56	1,903.89	3,507.27	387.09	3,894.36	1,990.47	44,181.48

Table 7 – Continued from previous page. . .

Year	Ending FAST Balance	FAST Fee	Social Security Commitment Net FAST	New Healthcare Borrowing	Total Annual PFA Borrowing	Total Annual PFA Borrowing Net FAST Fee	Cumulative Net FAST Borrowing
2042	102,893.60	2,099.87	3,413.39	366.42	3,779.81	1,679.94	45,861.42
2043	113,259.34	2,311.42	3,292.83	359.24	3,652.07	1,340.65	47,202.07
2044	124,428.08	2,539.35	3,172.45	336.14	3,508.59	969.24	48,171.31
2045	136,442.93	2,784.55	3,030.60	305.96	3,336.56	552.01	48,723.32
2046	149,357.53	3,048.11	2,874.84	266.76	3,141.60	93.49	48,816.81
2047	163,227.49	3,331.17	2,696.96	241.19	2,938.15	-393.02	48,423.79
2048	178,105.86	3,634.81	2,495.88	212.26	2,708.14	-926.67	47,497.12
2049	194,051.83	3,960.24	2,246.41	211.96	2,458.37	-1,501.87	45,995.25
2050	211,112.43	4,308.42	1,988.45	185.71	2,174.16	-2,134.26	43,860.99
2051	229,367.37	4,680.97	1,856.39	157.33	2,013.72	-2,667.25	41,193.74
2052	248,867.42	5,078.93	1,689.10	130.21	1,819.31	-3,259.62	37,934.12
2053	269,672.39	5,503.52	1,486.77	106.25	1,593.02	-3,910.50	34,023.62
2054	291,841.89	5,955.96	1,242.23	80.10	1,322.33	-4,633.63	29,389.99
2055	315,421.91	6,437.18	900.00	101.45	1,001.45	-5,435.73	23,954.26
2056	340,477.55	6,948.52	569.89	68.56	638.45	-6,310.07	17,644.19
2057	367,089.28	7,491.62	194.08	43.33	237.41	-7,254.21	10,389.98
2058	395,318.60	8,067.73	-231.97	17.50	-214.47	-8,282.20	2,107.78
2059	425,270.90	8,679.00	-684.51	-11.05	-695.56	-9,374.56	-7,266.78
2060	457,009.90	9,326.73	-1,275.91	27.70	-1,248.21	-10,574.94	-17,841.72
2061	490,613.52	10,012.52	-1,842.10	-17.19	-1,859.29	-11,871.81	-29,713.53
2062	526,139.62	10,737.54	-2,501.56	-49.94	-2,551.50	-13,289.04	-43,002.57
2063	563,650.72	11,503.08	-3,243.11	-75.62	-3,318.73	-14,821.81	-57,824.38
2064	603,228.65	12,310.79	-4,058.51	-100.70	-4,159.21	-16,470.00	-74,294.38
2065	644,918.75	13,161.61	-4,981.56	-130.30	-5,111.86	-18,273.47	-92,567.85
2066	688,807.16	14,057.29	-6,083.63	-54.74	-6,138.37	-20,195.66	-112,763.51
2067	734,991.32	14,999.82	-7,116.72	-113.89	-7,230.61	-22,230.43	-134,993.94
2068	783,575.45	15,991.34	-8,246.60	-151.33	-8,397.93	-24,389.27	-159,383.21
2069	834,661.61	17,033.91	-9,454.42	-190.58	-9,645.00	-26,678.91	-186,062.12
2070	888,407.07	18,130.76	-10,717.56	-215.86	-10,933.42	-29,064.18	-215,126.30
2071	944,874.95	19,283.16	-12,114.80	-239.05	-12,353.85	-31,637.01	-246,763.31
2072	1,004,138.25	20,492.62	-13,787.25	-114.15	-13,901.40	-34,394.02	-281,157.33
2073	1,066,362.26	21,762.50	-15,296.46	-206.26	-15,502.72	-37,265.22	-318,422.55

Table 7 – *Continued from previous page...*

Year	Ending FAST Balance	FAST Fee	Social Security Commitment Net FAST	New Healthcare Borrowing	Total Annual PFA Borrowing	Total Annual PFA Borrowing Net FAST Fee	Cumulative Net FAST Borrowing
2074	1,131,678.42	23,095.48	-16,952.43	-243.92	-17,196.35	-40,291.83	-358,714.38
2075	1,200,328.57	24,496.50	-18,637.83	-273.88	-18,911.71	-43,408.21	-402,122.59
2076	1,272,467.77	25,968.73	-20,449.94	-281.75	-20,731.69	-46,700.42	-448,823.01
2077	1,348,254.72	27,515.40	-22,353.10	-305.53	-22,658.63	-50,174.03	-498,997.04
2078	1,427,861.85	29,140.04	-24,561.78	-133.36	-24,695.14	-53,835.18	-552,832.22
2079	1,511,473.97	30,846.41	-26,586.49	-251.60	-26,838.09	-57,684.50	-610,516.72
2080	1,599,274.30	32,638.25	-28,805.31	-299.24	-29,104.55	-61,742.80	-672,259.52
2081	1,691,439.36	34,519.17	-31,179.90	-331.35	-31,511.25	-66,030.42	-738,289.94
2082	1,788,185.93	36,493.59	-33,691.67	-358.03	-34,049.70	-70,543.29	-808,833.23
2083	1,889,699.74	38,565.30	-36,393.54	-355.16	-36,748.70	-75,314.00	-884,147.23
2084	1,996,186.23	40,738.49	-39,456.92	-139.40	-39,596.32	-80,334.81	-964,482.04
2085	2,107,877.59	43,017.91	-42,314.44	-290.19	-42,604.63	-85,622.54	-1,050,104.58
2086	2,225,011.01	45,408.39	-45,457.96	-313.93	-45,771.89	-91,180.28	-1,141,284.86
2087	2,347,854.57	47,915.40	-48,770.91	-322.41	-49,093.32	-97,008.72	-1,238,293.58
2088	2,476,565.11	50,542.15	-52,353.45	-323.29	-52,676.74	-103,218.89	-1,341,512.47
2089	2,611,453.62	53,294.97	-56,293.59	-124.02	-56,417.61	-109,712.58	-1,451,225.05
2090	2,752,783.62	56,179.26	-60,106.90	-265.30	-60,372.20	-116,551.46	-1,567,776.51
2091	2,900,882.53	59,201.68	-64,209.12	-292.40	-64,501.52	-123,703.20	-1,691,479.71
2092	3,056,022.24	62,367.80	-68,571.23	-294.19	-68,865.42	-131,233.22	-1,822,712.93
2093	3,218,545.89	65,684.61	-73,139.90	-292.47	-73,432.37	-139,116.98	-1,961,829.91
2094	3,388,831.70	69,159.83	-77,919.23	-284.56	-78,203.79	-147,363.62	-2,109,193.53
2095	3,567,243.34	72,800.88	-83,105.46	-108.10	-83,213.56	-156,014.44	-2,265,207.97
2096	3,754,032.92	76,612.92	-88,351.74	-221.84	-88,573.58	-165,186.50	-2,430,394.47
2097	3,949,587.79	80,603.83	-93,955.72	-237.86	-94,193.58	-174,797.41	-2,605,191.88
2098	4,154,330.46	84,782.25	-99,829.07	-234.34	-100,063.41	-184,845.66	-2,790,037.54
2099	4,368,696.93	89,157.08	-105,989.36	-224.31	-106,213.67	-195,370.75	-2,985,408.29
2100	4,593,100.04	93,736.74	-112,476.30	-217.77	-112,694.07	-206,430.81	-3,191,839.10

Table 8: *PFA Impact on the Government Assuming 10.2% Market Return*

This table contains the projected PFA impact on the Federal Government of the United State of America. "Year" indicates the year to which the data correspond. "Federal Deficit" is the projected Federal Deficit under current environment. "Total Federal Surplus (PFA)" represents the amount of surplus the Federal Government would run if PFA were enacted and fully implemented, including interest on any debt issued to support PFA and benefit once the FAST Fee can be distributed to the government. "Total Federal Surplus (PFA with Excess FAST Fee)" represents the Federal Surplus when the FAST Fee is applied back to the Federal Government budget after it has completely covered all borrowing of the plan. "Federal Debt Held by the Public" is the amount of debt the Federal Government is expected to carry under the current environment. "FAST Fee" is the annual 2% management fee. "Total PFA Borrowing Net Fast Fee" is the amount of PFA borrowing that would need to be funded by outside sources after using the Fast fee as a source of capital. See page 4 for a discussion on the jagged nature of these projections. All values are reported in billions of dollars.

Year	Total Federal Deficit	Federal Debt Held by the Public	Total Federal Surplus (PFA)	Total Federal Surplus (PFA with Excess FAST Fee)	FAST Fee	Total PFA Borrowing Net FAST Fee
2020	1,000.00	17,900.00	-27.60	-27.60	27.87	1,930.54
2021	1,000.00	18,900.00	35.00	35.00	58.87	3,875.45
2022	1,100.00	20,100.00	288.40	288.40	93.25	6,013.29
2023	1,100.00	21,200.00	288.40	288.40	131.30	8,092.47
2024	1,200.00	22,500.00	188.40	188.40	173.27	10,103.36
2025	1,300.00	23,800.00	88.40	88.40	219.46	12,034.89
2026	1,300.00	25,200.00	780.00	780.00	270.23	14,316.27
2027	1,300.00	26,500.00	780.00	780.00	326.00	16,514.60
2028	1,500.00	28,200.00	580.00	580.00	387.12	18,601.96
2029	1,500.00	29,700.00	580.00	580.00	453.97	20,587.24
2030	1,700.00	31,400.00	380.00	380.00	527.01	22,457.59
2031	1,900.00	33,400.00	1,839.20	1,839.20	606.75	25,214.08
2032	2,100.00	35,500.00	1,639.20	1,639.20	693.74	27,839.84
2033	2,200.00	37,700.00	1,539.20	1,539.20	788.52	30,311.18
2034	2,400.00	40,200.00	1,339.20	1,339.20	891.57	32,612.27
2035	2,600.00	42,800.00	1,139.20	1,139.20	1,003.43	34,735.68
2036	2,800.00	45,700.00	939.20	939.20	1,124.84	36,670.68
2037	3,100.00	48,700.00	639.20	639.20	1,256.64	38,405.89
2038	3,300.00	52,000.00	439.20	439.20	1,399.61	39,924.82
2039	3,600.00	55,600.00	139.20	139.20	1,554.57	41,188.55
2040	3,800.00	59,400.00	-60.80	-60.80	1,722.37	42,191.01
2041	4,100.00	63,500.00	2,120.80	2,120.80	1,903.89	44,181.48
2042	4,400.00	67,900.00	1,820.80	1,820.80	2,099.87	45,861.42
2043	4,700.00	72,700.00	1,520.80	1,520.80	2,311.42	47,202.07
2044	5,100.00	77,700.00	1,120.80	1,120.80	2,539.35	48,171.31
2045	5,400.00	83,100.00	820.80	820.80	2,784.55	48,723.32
2046	5,800.00	89,000.00	420.80	420.80	3,048.11	48,816.81
2047	6,200.00	95,200.00	20.80	20.80	3,331.17	48,423.79
2048	6,700.00	101,800.00	-479.20	-479.20	3,634.81	47,497.12
2049	7,100.00	109,000.00	-879.20	-879.20	3,960.24	45,995.25
2050	7,700.00	116,600.00	-1,479.20	-1,479.20	4,308.42	43,860.99

Table 8 – *Continued from previous page...*

Year	Total Federal Deficit	Federal Debt Held by the Public	Total Federal Surplus (PFA)	Total Federal Surplus (PFA with Excess FAST Fee)	FAST Fee	Total PFA Borrowing Net FAST Fee
2051	7,929.60	120,960.00	-1,488.00	-1,488.00	4,680.97	41,193.74
2052	8,224.60	125,460.00	-1,552.60	-1,552.60	5,078.93	37,934.12
2053	8,519.60	129,960.00	-1,607.60	-1,607.60	5,503.52	34,023.62
2054	8,826.40	134,640.00	-1,674.40	-1,674.40	5,955.96	29,389.99
2055	9,145.00	139,500.00	-1,743.40	-1,743.40	6,437.18	23,954.26
2056	9,475.40	144,540.00	-1,814.60	-1,814.60	6,948.52	17,644.19
2057	9,817.60	149,760.00	-1,888.00	-1,888.00	7,491.62	10,389.98
2058	10,171.60	155,160.00	-1,963.60	-1,963.60	8,067.73	2,107.78
2059	10,537.40	160,740.00	-2,041.40	6,637.60	8,679.00	-7,266.78
2060	10,926.80	166,680.00	-2,133.20	7,193.53	9,326.73	-17,841.72
2061	11,328.00	172,800.00	-2,227.20	7,785.32	10,012.52	-29,713.53
2062	11,741.00	179,100.00	-2,323.40	8,414.14	10,737.54	-43,002.57
2063	12,165.80	185,580.00	-2,412.20	9,090.88	11,503.08	-57,824.38
2064	12,614.20	192,420.00	-2,515.00	9,795.79	12,310.79	-74,294.38
2065	13,074.40	199,440.00	-2,620.00	10,541.61	13,161.61	-92,567.85
2066	13,546.40	206,640.00	-2,727.20	11,330.09	14,057.29	-112,763.51
2067	14,042.00	214,200.00	-2,838.80	12,161.02	14,999.82	-134,993.94
2068	14,549.40	221,940.00	-2,952.60	13,038.74	15,991.34	-159,383.21
2069	15,080.40	230,040.00	-3,070.80	13,963.11	17,033.91	-186,062.12
2070	15,635.00	238,500.00	-3,203.00	14,927.76	18,130.76	-215,126.30
2071	16,201.40	247,140.00	-3,327.80	15,955.36	19,283.16	-246,763.31
2072	16,791.40	256,140.00	-3,466.60	17,026.02	20,492.62	-281,157.33
2073	17,405.00	265,500.00	-3,609.80	18,152.70	21,762.50	-318,422.55
2074	18,042.20	275,220.00	-3,757.40	19,338.08	23,095.48	-358,714.38
2075	18,703.00	285,300.00	-3,909.40	20,587.10	24,496.50	-402,122.59
2076	19,387.40	295,740.00	-4,075.40	21,893.33	25,968.73	-448,823.01
2077	20,095.40	306,540.00	-4,245.80	23,269.60	27,515.40	-498,997.04
2078	20,827.00	317,700.00	-4,420.60	24,719.44	29,140.04	-552,832.22
2079	21,582.20	329,220.00	-4,599.80	26,246.61	30,846.41	-610,516.72
2080	22,372.80	341,280.00	-4,795.20	27,843.05	32,638.25	-672,259.52
2081	23,187.00	353,700.00	-4,985.40	29,533.77	34,519.17	-738,289.94
2082	24,036.60	366,660.00	-5,191.80	31,301.79	36,493.59	-808,833.23
2083	24,909.80	379,980.00	-5,402.60	33,162.70	38,565.30	-884,147.23
2084	25,818.40	393,840.00	-5,620.00	35,118.49	40,738.49	-964,482.04
2085	26,762.40	408,240.00	-5,853.60	37,164.31	43,017.91	-1,050,104.58
2086	27,741.80	423,180.00	-6,093.80	39,314.59	45,408.39	-1,141,284.86
2087	28,756.60	438,660.00	-6,340.60	41,574.80	47,915.40	-1,238,293.58
2088	29,806.80	454,680.00	-6,603.60	43,938.55	50,542.15	-1,341,512.47
2089	30,892.40	471,240.00	-6,873.20	46,421.77	53,294.97	-1,451,225.05
2090	32,025.20	488,520.00	-7,161.20	49,018.06	56,179.26	-1,567,776.51
2091	33,193.40	506,340.00	-7,455.80	51,745.88	59,201.68	-1,691,479.71
2092	34,408.80	524,880.00	-7,759.20	54,608.60	62,367.80	-1,822,712.93
2093	35,659.60	543,960.00	-8,069.20	57,615.41	65,684.61	-1,961,829.91

Table 8 – *Continued from previous page...*

Year	Total Federal Deficit	Federal Debt Held by the Public	Total Federal Surplus (PFA)	Total Federal Surplus (PFA with Excess FAST Fee)	FAST Fee	Total PFA Borrowing Net FAST Fee
2094	36,957.60	563,760.00	-8,397.60	60,762.23	69,159.83	-2,109,193.53
2095	38,302.80	584,280.00	-8,734.80	64,066.08	72,800.88	-2,265,207.97
2096	39,707.00	605,700.00	-9,092.60	67,520.32	76,612.92	-2,430,394.47
2097	41,158.40	627,840.00	-9,459.20	71,144.63	80,603.83	-2,605,191.88
2098	42,657.00	650,700.00	-9,834.60	74,947.65	84,782.25	-2,790,037.54
2099	44,214.60	674,460.00	-10,230.60	78,926.48	89,157.08	-2,985,408.29
2100	45,831.20	699,120.00	-10,647.20	83,089.54	93,736.74	-3,191,839.10

Authors

Terry Nager

Eric Nager

Kyre Dane Lahtinen

For further information:

www.PlanForAmerica.us

Made in the USA
Monee, IL
03 July 2021